TOP POT HAND-FORGED DOUGHNUTS

TOP POT HAND-FORGED
DOUGHNUTS

Secrets and Recipes for the Home Baker

By Mark and Michael Klebeck
with Jess Thomson

Photographs by Scott Pitts

CHRONICLE BOOKS
SAN FRANCISCO

Library of Congress Cataloging-in-
Publication Data available.

ISBN 978-1-4521-0212-2
Manufactured in China.

Designed by Patrick Nistler

Food styling by Charlotte Omnès

The photographer wishes to thank his wife,
Meghan, for her constant support and endless
patience, Mark Klebeck, Michael Klebeck,
E.J. Armstrong, Norm, and Tony Burlison.

Photos on pages 2, 8, 12, and 140 © Mark Klebeck

Bob's Red Mill gluten-free all-purpose flour is a
registered trademark of Bob's Red Mill Natural
Foods Inc.; Guinness is a registered trademark
of Guinness & Co.; Oregon Chai is a registered
trademark of Oregon Chai, Inc. and WorldPantry.
com, Inc.; Pop Rocks is a registered trademark of
Zeta Especial S.A.

10 9 8 7 6 5 4 3 2 1

Chronicle Books
680 Second Street
San Francisco, California 94107
www.chroniclebooks.com

Michael Klebeck would like to thank:

God, August and June Klebeck; beautiful Georgette, Lucy, Louise, and Ulysses Klebeck; Terri and Martin Chacon; the entire Klebeck Family, brothers, sisters, uncles, aunts, nephews, nieces, cousins, in-laws, etc.; special thanks to Norm Day, the Hardwick family, Bill T., all the Top Pot extended family, including office staff, bakers, baristas, drivers, and roasters; all the artists and crafts people who helped make Top Pot so beautiful; special thanks to Russ R. and Maggie Cole for God's sake; Tina R.; Todd H.; Kent I.; and the Lorig crew (Russ H., Joel G., Beau H., Matt C., and Todd H., again!!); Kris von Oy, the Pilkey family, Father Squier, Father Daniel Syverstad O.P.; Blessed Sacrament; the entire A.S.B. students, families, and staff; Saint Francis Cabrini, Lakewood, Wedgwood, and Seattle for making Top Pot so amazing and successful; Joel Radin and his family; Bryan Yeck; the early coffee crews at Bauhaus, Zeitgeist, and Top Pot; the early and current investors who believed and still believe!! Last, but not least, Mark K., Jess Thomson, and the entire Chronicle Books family!

Mark Klebeck would like to thank:

My parents, August and June Klebeck; my wife Libby, for her endless love and support; our sons Wolfgang and Otto—that they, too, will be fortunate to grow up and figure out what it is that they love to do in life; my brother Michael who I had the best time designing and building stores with, who inspired me, and who has more guts than anyone I have ever met; my entire Klebeck family; the Fernau family from Stevensville "the polka capital of the world" Michigan; Bill Terhar, a great friend and leader who tirelessly motivated me and drove Top Pot to success; Alex Sharma for believing in the company from day one; Tony Walker and family; Phyllis Hatfield; all our shareholders who believed in us; Tom Douglas for being such a great supporter, colleague, and 5th Avenue neighbor; my friend Brian Miller—Wide Angle TV; Tracy Dethlefs at Hullabaloo TV; Juanita Clemente; Dave and Dana Dysart; Chris Ballew; John Richards and everyone at KEXP; the city of Lakewood, Washington; King of Hawaii; the Wexley School for Girls; Dandy Social Club.

The artists: Tina Randolph, Matt Shoudy, Russ Rasmussen, Norman Day, Todd Hardman, Christine Godlewski, Art Chantry, and Ed Fotheringham; Scott Pitts for his photographic talents and mentoring; Amy Gundlach; *Seattle Met Magazine; Alaska Airlines Magazine*; Jessica Shambora at *Fortune* magazine; Andy Rothman at CNBC; the Travel Channel; Mark DeCarlo; Allison Dalvit at Food Network Challenge for pushing me to compete! Amy Clancy; Steve Wilson; Ben Saboonchian; Bret Stetka; John T. Edge; John Riordan; Jane and Michael Stern; NPR; KUOW; Julien Perry, Lori Harris at SBUX—you will always be remembered for your friendship and dedication to Top Pot from day one; Josh Brower and Jerry Nagae for your guidance and for always watching out for us during this great ride! Frank Burklund and all the Top Pot Doughnut bakers—present and past—you are so appreciated! To Gina Mainwal and Kim Yamagiwa, who led the charge early on; to our front counter staff, delivery drivers, and vendors; Joel Radin—co-founder and friend; Bryan Yeck and the staff at Zeitgeist Coffee; Belshaw Brothers; O.B. Williams; Visions Espresso; and the hundreds of GREAT suppliers.

Special thanks to Jess Thomson for her months of work putting this book together; Lorena Jones at Chronicle Books for always checking in and pushing me to make this happen; TO SEATTLE WASHINGTON USA! You made this happen and we could not have done it without you!

To EVERYONE else inadvertently not mentioned— THANK YOU!

CONTENTS

We weren't bakers or pastry chefs before we started Top Pot Doughnuts—just two brothers who liked a good business plan and the occasional Monday morning doughnut. Over the years, along with our team of bakers, we've developed the doughnuts Top Pot has made famous. In this book, we've collected all the knowledge we've amassed—doughnut-making tips and tricks, the best classic flavor combinations, and ideas for outside-the-box doughnuts—and translated it into recipes designed with the home cook in mind. From traditional spiced and devil's food cake doughnuts to yeast-raised and old-fashioned ones, with variations for bars, bismarks, twists, and fritters, *Top Pot Hand-Forged Doughnuts* passes our recipes on.

TOP POT: A BRIEF HISTORY

At Top Pot, we make about 1.3 million doughnuts every week. In rough numbers, that's enough glazed goodness to stretch doughnuts end to end for ten miles every day. But we didn't start big. In fact, when we opened our first doughnut shop on Seattle's Capitol Hill in 2002, we didn't even have doughnuts. But we're getting ahead of ourselves.

Top Pot started with a sign. In 1996, a few years after we'd opened a coffee shop called Zeitgeist in Seattle's Pioneer Square, we found a giant neon sign from a defunct Chinese restaurant that read "TOPSPOT." We bought it for $400 and stored it in our mother's backyard in North Seattle for five years, where it slowly began succumbing to rust and raccoons.

Meanwhile, Zeitgeist boomed. Built with a midcentury German design aesthetic and a high-end clientele in mind, the shop sold excellent house-roasted coffee and fancy pastries. There was just one problem: Each Monday, one of our pastry purveyors was closed, so we never had enough breakfast foods. We started passing by a local doughnut shop before opening on Mondays, just to have something to fill our pastry case, and noticed that, with astounding regularity, the doughnuts were the first to go. We might have eaten a few ourselves.

In 2000, Michael found a great deal on some used doughnut-making equipment—a kettle fryer, the depositor used for cake doughnuts, a proofing rack, and a big stainless steel work table—thinking we might someday learn to make our own. The same year, Zeitgeist moved to a new location, and we started baking our own quick breads and muffins. We hoped to add doughnuts to the list of housemade goods, but the equipment didn't fit in the new space. We squirreled it away in the shop we'd just leased on Summit Avenue in Capitol Hill that was intended to be Zeitgeist II, thinking we'd found a temporary solution.

Then we hit upon the idea of opening a doughnut shop, making them by hand rather than depending on the machines the large, increasingly popular doughnut shops were using. Following the same design philosophy we captured at Zeitgeist, and before that at another coffee shop called Bauhaus, we decided to name our new place Top Spot and to front it with the rickety old neon sign. Before becoming coffee entrepreneurs, we had been general contractors, and between us, we had years of experience in remodeling, building cabinetry, and designing restaurant spaces. So we built out the cafe ourselves, pouring the terrazzo floors and building the bookcases—now a signature trimming at Top Pot's cafes—one shelf at a time. But the day we drove the sign down Interstate 5 in Michael's 1966 Ford F-100, there was a rattle and a loud clunk as the "S" fell off the rusty old sign— and Top Pot Doughnuts was born.

When the Summit Avenue store opened, things were a little hectic. We had the doughnut-frying equipment but no doughnut-making experience. We knew doughnuts were special; as the last two of eight kids, we would often get to go with our mother to a doughnut shop in Tacoma called The Golden Oven for twists, as a special treat when she had time with just the two of us. We felt we could create a doughnut that was more artisanal and more gourmet than what was out there, hand culling each batch, and frying and glazing in small batches rather than relying on conveyor belts and machines to churn out doughnuts no human hands had touched. We thought, "How hard could it be?"

For the first month, while we sold the same muffins, bagels, and scones we'd had at Zeitgeist, we learned how to make doughnuts. We made mistakes. But since the beginning, accidents have been a crucial part of the process and, we believe, of our success. We didn't want to make the same doughnuts those other guys made, so we tinkered and played, crafting doughnut after doughnut by hand until we found versions that fitted our creative personalities—hence our slogan, "Hand-Forged Doughnuts." We talked to our customers and realized that even though about 80 percent of the doughnuts made in the United States were raised (yeast) doughnuts, people wanted more cake doughnuts. So we made more cake. A month later, without the help of a single doughnut expert, we had doughnuts we loved.

Once we started actually selling them, word about Top Pot Doughnuts spread quickly. Seattle-ites poured in from all over the city, packing dozens away for soccer games, parties, and meetings. The line snaked out the door. In the fall of 2003, we opened our flagship store on Fifth Avenue, right in downtown Seattle, outfitted with a neon bucking bronco sign, huge, two-story tall greenhouse windows, a bakery big enough to produce doughnuts for multiple stores, and a coffee-roasting room. It immediately became not just a neighborhood habit for locals, but also an essential stop on Seattle's tourist routes.

One morning shortly after it opened, Howard Schultz, chairman and CEO of Starbucks, visited the Fifth Avenue store. He ordered a variety dozen, and apparently loved them. Fast forward to 2005: We started working with Starbucks to bake doughnuts for their stores—first just in western Washington, then across the Pacific Northwest, and then across the United States.

In the years that followed, we opened four more doughnut cafes in Seattle's Wedgwood, Queen Anne, Bellevue, and Mill Creek neighborhoods. We designed and built each ourselves. At each location, Top Pot cafes mimic our doughnut style—creatively but simply decorated and totally self-inspired.

Top Pot Doughnuts are now sold in Seattle, in 14,000 Starbucks stores, in Whole Foods Markets in the Pacific Northwest, and in airports and coffee shops across the United States. In 2009, we equipped a 1962 Airstream Bambi with racks that hold 100 dozen doughnuts and joined the mobile food truck mania, hawking doughnuts at events across the city. In 2010, we signed an exclusive deal with Seattle's Qwest Stadium, becoming the doughnut provider for Seattle Seahawks and Seattle Sounders games.

With attractive decorations and smart names—like Pink Feather Boa, Valley Girl Lemon, and Double Trouble, to name just a few favorites—our doughnuts appeal to people because they're delicious and a bit nostalgic, and because they pair exceptionally well with coffee. If you can, come to one of our

shops to watch folks pick out their doughnuts. Conversations stop, and grown-ups peer into the case with the intensity usually reserved for choosing an engagement ring—even President Obama gawked a little when he visited in the fall of 2010.

Today, Top Pot is the only American doughnut company both small enough to maintain artisanal, small-batch quality and a vintage mom-and-pop aesthetic *and* big enough to produce doughnuts available worldwide.

And now you can "hand-forge" them at home.

THE TOP POT BAKERY

Hidden in an old warehouse on Fifth Avenue, right in downtown Seattle, Top Pot's bakery produces more than 75 million doughnuts each year. We put our cake and old-fashioned doughnut batter in a giant hopper, which our bakers use to deposit forty doughnuts a minute into baths of hot oil that probably rival the size of your dining room table. There are no doughnut-flipping machines, as there are at many doughnut companies—each one is still turned by hand at just the right moment—and each of our yeast-raised doughnuts is still cut, formed, and glazed by hand. Every baker has his or her own technique: they slide the frying racks into the oil a certain way, or rotate their wrists to pop the doughnuts out of the chocolate icing a bit differently, and they all have their personal favorites.

But our bakers also all have two things in common: dedication and speed. The first allows us to trust our employees to provide each of our customers with a doughnut that meets our stringent standards. (Our bakery runs around the clock.) The second lets us produce an impressive volume with relatively few bakers.

Unfortunately, we can't send our bakers or our equipment home with you, which means that there are a few things that will be different about your homemade doughnuts. For one, they'll be smaller than ours, so that at home, in your deep fryer or a simple frying pan, you can cook more than one at a time. We've changed the proofing process for yeast-raised doughnuts to a home-kitchen-friendly method. We offer icings and glazes that don't use agar, the natural stabilizing agent we use to prevent the icings from weeping, because they're simply easier to work with. Finally, we've narrowed down our ingredients to things you should be able to find in a large grocery store and a good kitchen supply store. (Just in case, we have provided a list of resources on page 140 for everything you'll need.)

Have fun. Our bakers sure do.

A DOUGHNUT HISTORY
and
PRIMER

The Merriam-Webster dictionary defines a doughnut as "a small, usually ring-shaped cake fried in fat." We can't argue with that, but as is the case with most foods, there's more to the story—where the doughnut originated, how it became a comfort food, and why it's enjoying such a resurgence today.

In *Glazed America: A History of the Doughnut*, author Paul R. Mullins says the word *doughnut* is attributed to Washington Irving, who used "dough nut" to describe deep-fried balls of sweetened dough, and compared them to similar Dutch treats called *olykoeks*.

Since almost every culture has some form of sweet fried dough—traces of fried doughnut-shaped cakes were found in Native American caves, and the Bible clearly refers to the use of fried cakes as an offering—it's difficult to pinpoint where the modern doughnut originated. According to John T. Edge, author of *Donuts: An American Passion*, some food historians track the American doughnut trade back to a Dutch New Yorker, who opened a doughnut shop in Manhattan in 1776, selling *olykoeks* and coffee in the financial district. Doughnuts started showing up in cookbooks in the early 19th century and reached their first peak of popularity in the 1920s. According to Edge, the alternative spelling "donut" was invented when the New York–based Doughnut Machine Corporation abbreviated the word to make it more pronounceable by the foreigners they hoped would buy their automated doughnut-making equipment.

But although it's widely accepted that the modern doughnut originated with the Dutch, just how it became so popular in America is a subject of some debate. According to one theory, when the Salvation Army dispatched women to Europe during World War I to comfort and care for the troops there, the "lassies," as they were called, made dozens upon dozens of doughnuts. Edge writes:

Though contemporary accounts differ as to how and why, there is no doubt that their decision to fry donuts would transform fried dough from a vaguely foreign food, loosely associated with the Dutch, into a symbol of American home and hearth, a gustatory manifestation of the ideals for which the soldiers fought . . . When American soldiers got home from World War I, they arrived with a taste for, among other goods, French wine and filterless cigarettes. But no acquisition would affect the way Americans ate as would their taste for donuts.

Veterans opened doughnut shops. Doughnuts moved from being a homemade goodie to an almost uniquely store-bought treat. Doughnut shops became de facto community centers, places where people could go to gossip, fuel up on coffee, and break up their day.

As mass production became the norm across the food industry and people became increasingly mobile, Americans developed an even stronger taste for goods produced outside the home. Over the course of the 1950s and '60s, when American car ownership boomed, people started buying doughnuts on the go, at drive-throughs and gas stations. Doughnut chains expanded, and doughnuts became a quintessential American icon.

Doughnut sales languished in the latter part of the 20th century, but today America is in the grips of a doughnut renaissance. Spawned by a recession that increased sales in comforting consumables, such as junk food, beer, and—you guessed it—doughnuts, the boom has inched its way across the foodie world, too, starting with high-end restaurants, where doughnuts began appearing in fancier forms on dessert menus a few years ago. Today, designer doughnut stores are blanketing cities, brides are choosing doughnuts over traditional wedding cakes, and the eating public is replacing its cupcake craving with a soft spot for boutique bakeries that take the doughnut concept to the next level, with creative flavors and coffee lounge atmospheres. And Top Pot's right out in front.

TYPES OF DOUGHNUTS

At Top Pot, we make three basic types of doughnuts: cake (vanilla, spiced, and chocolate), yeast-raised, and old-fashioned. Though their ingredients and preparation differ, they're all quite manageable at home. Can't decide where to start? We suggest cake doughnuts with a simple icing, because they require the least amount of time and attention.

Cake Doughnuts

Made with cake/soft-wheat flour to keep them light-textured, and plenty of nutmeg for Top Pot's signature flavor, these doughnuts are the best choice for creative decorators. Our version is a bit crispier on the outside than those you'll find in big-box doughnut shops. For our devil's food cake doughnuts, we use Dutch-processed cocoa for a deep, rich chocolate flavor.

Yeast-Raised Doughnuts

Bread/strong flour makes our yeast-raised doughnuts pleasantly chewy, and the yeast makes them airy. At Top Pot, we let our mace-spiked raised doughnut dough rise in a warm, moist proofing oven big enough to fit a small car. Since you probably don't have one of those, we've devised a foolproof rising technique that yields rings, bars, and fritters very much like the ones you'll find in our stores.

Old-Fashioned Doughnuts

The signature split on the top of a rich, tangy old-fashioned doughnut—our bakers call the ring in the center the doughnut's "ridge" and the split sections on the outside its "petals"—shows up because we make them with a bit of extra leavening and sour cream, and fry them at a lower temperature using a special technique, flipping them twice instead of just once.

A GLOSSARY OF DOUGHNUT INGREDIENTS

Although many of the ingredients in this book will be familiar to you, there are some you may not have seen before, such as agar, and some you may feel compelled to use substitutes for, like cake/soft-wheat flour. Our recipes were developed with your success at home in mind. We recommend using the appropriate ingredients. **Also, we use the spoon-and-level method to measure all dry ingredients, but whenever possible, we suggest weighing them.**

Agar: This is a stabilizing agent, derived from sea-weed, that is tasteless and colorless. At Top Pot, we use it in all our glazes and icings to make them set, so our final product is less fragile. However, it does set very quickly, which means glazes and icings made with agar must be used immediately or reheated before application. For information on using agar, see "Icing and Glazing Tips" on page 29.

Bread/strong flour: Because yeast-raised dough-nuts should have a bit of chew, we use bread/strong flour, which has a higher protein content—and thus more gluten—than all-purpose/plain flour.

Butter: Although butter is very useful in most baking, we don't use a lot of it in our doughnut recipes. However, if you must, use an unsalted butter, because there's already salt in our recipes.

Cake/soft-wheat flour: Made from wheat that's lower in protein, cake/soft-wheat flour results in an end product that's more tender than it would be if made with all-purpose/plain flour. If you can't find it, make it: For every cup of all-purpose/plain flour used in a recipe, substitute 2 tbsp cornstarch/cornflour for 2 tbsp of the flour. Always sift cake/soft-wheat flour after measuring.

Canola oil: We recommend canola oil for frying at home. For more information on frying oils, see page 25.

Cocoa powder: Dutch-processed cocoa powder is processed with an alkalizing agent; it has a stronger flavor that we like for our devil's food cake dough-nuts. Natural cocoa powder will also work, but the chocolate flavor won't be as pronounced.

Confectioners'/icing sugar: Confectioners'/icing sugar, also known as powdered sugar, is often quite clumpy, so it needs to be sifted before making glazes or icings. Always sift confectioners'/icing sugar after measuring.

Corn/golden syrup: Light corn/golden syrup improves the texture and shine of our glazes and icings and prevents sugar crystals from forming in the glazes and icings as they cool.

Gluten-free all-purpose baking flour: Sold in small bags in the baking or gluten-free aisles of many large supermarkets, gluten-free flour can be used in place of regular wheat flours when making gluten-free doughnuts.

Mace: Used only in our yeast-raised doughnuts, ground mace is a spice made from the outer layer of a nutmeg seed, with a slightly different taste. It gives yeast-raised doughnuts their unique flavor.

Nutmeg: This gives our spice cake doughnuts their signature flavor. For more spice flavor, substitute freshly grated nutmeg for the ground kind you find in your grocery store's baking aisle.

Salt: We use iodized salt, because its small granules allow for even dispersion.

Shortening/vegetable lard: Since butter contains water, it can cause doughnuts to split while frying. We find that shortening/vegetable lard, which has no water in it, works best for us. You can substitute butter, but your final product may not be quite the same. Look for a product free of trans fats.

Sour cream: Use full-fat sour cream for moist doughnuts.

Sugar: When we refer to sugar in this book, we mean regular white granulated sugar.

Vanilla extract: Real vanilla extract (as opposed to imitation vanilla) has the best flavor.

Yeast: We use regular active dry yeast, typically available in small packets or in glass jars. Yeast can lose its rising power over time, so we recommend buying fresh yeast for each batch.

DOUGHNUT-MAKING TOOLS

We got our start as carpenters, so we're familiar with the concept of having the right tool for the right job. However, much of the equipment required for doughnut making can be improvised. Here's what you'll need and what you can skip—and, in some cases, how you can improvise.

Bench scraper: Although a fat metal spatula without slots will work, a bench scraper, the metal tool many bakers use to cut and form dough, is quite useful in the doughnut-making process. Use it to lift cake doughnuts off your rolling surface and transfer them into hot oil, to move yeast-raised doughnuts without scarring them (see page 79), or to scrape dough off your cutting surface.

Cutter: A traditional doughnut cutter has two concentric rings, one 2³/₄ in/7 cm across and one 1¹/₄ in/3 cm in diameter. It's convenient, because you can punch out a doughnut and its hole in one motion, but it's not necessary. You can easily substitute a jam jar, a pickling jar, or a clean, empty tin can for the outside ring, and a smaller can or plastic bottle cap for the inside ring. Larger doughnut cutters work, but we find that it's difficult to fry more than one doughnut at a time in a home setting with

doughnuts that large. Alternatively, you can pick a doughnut recipe that doesn't require a cutter—try Maple Bars (page 83) or Classic Twists (page 75).

Deep fryer: Electric deep fryers maintain an even temperature for you, which makes the frying process much easier, but they're not required. See page 25 for tips on frying in one of the pans you have on hand.

Docker: A docker looks like a plastic 4-in/10-cm cylinder with plastic spikes on it; the spiky apparatus is attached to a handle so it rolls like a pizza cutter, leaving behind tons of tiny holes. At Top Pot, we roll it over the dough to poke holes in our yeast-raised bar, bismark, and bullseye doughs before the second rise, to prevent bubbles from forming in the dough during frying. You can use one, but it's not necessary.

Doughnut pans: With the exception of our Baked Raised Doughnuts (page 112), a doughnut pan is completely unnecessary—and even with those, it's not crucial. Skip this gadget.

Mesh strainer: At Top Pot, we proof and fry our yeast-raised doughnuts on large racks that can be completely submersed in the oil, which makes removing them easier—but chances are you don't have a similar set-up. Because they're more fragile, a large, round mesh strainer, such as the type found in many Asian markets, makes removing yeast-raised doughnuts (as well as any doughnut holes) a cinch. A large slotted spoon will also work.

Rolling pin: We use a classic rolling pin for rolling out dough, but an empty bottle of wine wrapped in plastic wrap/cling film also works nicely.

Stand mixer: We use a stand mixer—an electric mixer fitted with a large bowl that comes with a paddle attachment for mixing and a dough hook for kneading—for all our recipes. You can use a handheld electric mixer instead: For yeast-raised doughnuts, mix on medium speed with a handheld electric mixer until the dough becomes too firm to mix, then knead in the rest of the flour by hand and proceed as directed. For cake and old fashioned doughnuts, mix the dough on medium-low speed,

taking care not to mix past the point at which all of the flour has been incorporated—you don't want to overwork the dough—then refrigerate and proceed as directed. All glazes and icings can be whisked together by hand.

Thermometer: Because a difference of a few degrees in temperature can drastically affect the results when frying doughnuts, you'll need a deep-frying or candy thermometer (it's best to have one that clips to the side of your pot) that goes up to at least 400°F/200°C. Don't skip this. For more information on frying, see page 25.

Tongs: It's easiest to flip cake doughnuts with a pair of thin metal tongs, but you can use wooden (not plastic) chopsticks or the wrong end of two long metal spoons as well.

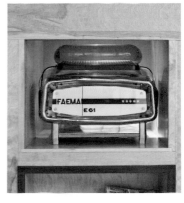

Hang around the bakery at our Fifth Avenue store for more than a few minutes, and you'll walk away with an education—every move is calculated and time-tested. And while each baker follows his or her own techniques when it comes to things like flipping dough-nuts or stirring icing, there are a few hard-and-fast rules that we watch every baker follow, which should also be heeded at home. Use the following tips for great homemade doughnuts.

Measure Correctly

To measure dry ingredients, such as flour and confectioners'/icing sugar, use the "spoon and level" method: first spoon the ingredient into the measuring cup, then level it with the back of a knife. Always sift ingredients after measuring.

Roll Out the Dough Evenly

When you roll out dough, do measure it with a ruler—1/2 in/12 mm may be thicker or thinner than you think. For simplicity, you can mark a toothpick or wooden skewer at the thickness you need, and poke it into the dough to judge its depth as you roll it out.

Cut Doughnuts Without a Mess

When you cut out doughnuts, flour the cutter itself, especially for sticky cake doughnut dough. To get the doughnut out of the cutter, tap the side of the cutter against the palm of your hand.

Proof Yeast-Raised Dough

Our oven-proofing method for yeast doughs adds warmth and moisture to the air around the dough. You can also let the dough rise in a warm place, leaving it covered for both rises instead of just the first rise, but it may take a bit longer. If you have a proofing box, use that instead of our method, letting the dough rise for about 45 minutes each time on the low setting.

Don't Always Double Recipes

Cake doughnut, old-fashioned doughnut, glaze, and icing recipes may be doubled, but yeast-raised recipes must be made in single batches, or the dough will climb out of the mixer during kneading.

Transport Doughnuts Gently

Although all doughnuts are best fresh, we realize that you may have to take them somewhere—and you might not have the same doughnut boxes we do. If you don't have a large, sealable container, line a shoebox or square-bottomed shopping bag with the top and handles cut off with waxed/greaseproof paper and stack the doughnuts inside (once the glaze or icing has dried completely), on their bottoms or sides.

FRYING DOUGHNUTS

Mention deep-frying anything at home, and many cooks panic. Hot oil requires care, of course, but doughnuts are simpler to make than you might think. If you have a deep fryer, consult the manufacturer's directions before beginning. Use fresh oil that comes up to the recommended level, usually about 3 in/7.5 cm above the frying basket. If you don't have one, don't worry— you can do it in a large, heavy-bottomed pan at home, using the following tips. Note that thermometers and stove settings vary; the times listed here are approximations.

Finding the Right Oil

At Top Pot, we fry in saturated fat-free palm oil, which starts as a solid. It gives a great flavor, and its solid state makes it easy to transport. But since it's not readily available for home use, we recommend frying in canola or vegetable oil, because it has a neutral flavor and because it can handle the temperatures used for doughnut frying.

If you have some on hand, peanut/groundnut oil, safflower oil, and corn oil are also suitable for frying doughnuts, but may leave a slight taste.

Coconut oil, hemp oil, olive oil, sesame oil, and lard will smoke at the temperatures called for in this book and should not be used.

Preparing Your Frying Space

It's true: Frying can be messy. But a few quick steps can make clean up a snap. Line the area around your frying pan with aluminum foil, and drain doughnuts on a cooling rack set over paper towels/absorbent paper, on top of the foil. Set all utensils on foil when they're not in use during frying.

Choosing a Vessel

Since doughnuts are less likely to break if they have plenty of room to be turned over, fry them in something you can fill with oil to a depth of *at least* 2 in/5 cm, *with at least* another 2 in/5 cm of room left at the top, so there's no risk that the oil will splash over the sides. However, using oil deeper than 4 in/10 cm will cause the doughnuts to take too long to float to the surface, and they may burn. Using a pot or pan with a smaller diameter will mean using less oil (and it will heat up more quickly), but it's often more difficult to turn the doughnuts when they're enclosed in a small space. In any case, choose a heavy-bottomed pot, so the oil heats evenly. See the chart in the next section for oil quantities.

Heating the Oil

It's important to give the oil enough time to heat up before you start frying. (See the chart that follows; keep in mind that times may vary depending on your stove.) Also note that the oil temperature may vary while you fry, so continue checking it as you go. Adjust your stove's setting often to maintain the desired temperature.

We highly recommend using a thermometer while frying, but if you can't find one, you'll know your oil is ready when you see vigorous convective motion along the bottom of the pan—almost like thin clouds moving quickly across the sky. But as we said, a thermometer is best.

Here are guidelines for heating oil over medium heat. You can rush it by heating it over a higher temperature, but that often results in oil that is hotter than the desired temperature.

Pan diameter:	**12 in/30 cm**
Oil required:	**12 cups/2.5 L**
Oil depth:	**2 in/5 cm**
Minimum pan height:	**4 in/10 cm**
Approximate time to heat to 325°F/165°C to 370°F/185°C:	**30 to 40 minutes**

Pan diameter:	**10 in/25 cm**
Oil required:	**10 cups/2.25 L**
Oil depth:	**2$\frac{1}{4}$ in/5.5 cm**
Minimum pan height:	**5 in/12.5 cm**
Approximate time to heat to 325°F/165°C to 370°F/185°C:	**25 to 35 minutes**

Pan diameter:	**8 in/20 cm**
Oil required:	**8 cups/2.5 L**
Oil depth:	**2$\frac{1}{2}$ in/6 cm**
Minimum pan height:	**5 in/12.5 cm**
Approximate time to heat to 325°F/165°C to 370°F/185°C:	**20 to 30 minutes**

For deep fryers, using oil up to the recommended level, approximate time to heat to 325°F/165°C to 370°F/185°C is 10 to 15 minutes.

Make a Sacrifice

You can use a scrap of doughnut dough, or a sacrificial doughnut, to test the oil. You may learn that the seconds go by quite quickly as you fry, or that the time it takes for your doughnuts to cook is slightly shorter or longer than listed in the recipe. Based on the first doughnut, use your judgment for the rest of the batch. Our cooking times are only approximations.

Turning Doughnuts

When turning doughnuts in hot oil, try to rotate them right at the oil's surface, using a pair of thin metal tongs or wooden chopsticks. Picking them up out of the oil will cause them to fall apart.

Frying Safety

Understandably, our instinct when working with sizzling oil is to move as quickly as possible. When frying doughnuts, though, moving slowly is best, because dropping doughnuts into hot oil makes the oil slosh out, which presents the possibility of a serious burn. To deposit doughnuts into the oil safely, slide them in on a metal spatula, or insert them by hand thin side first, letting go once about a third of the doughnut is immersed in the oil—dropping them in flat is dangerous. When removing doughnuts, let them drip briefly over the vat of oil before moving, to avoid flinging hot oil across your kitchen (or yourself).

And you've heard about oil and water, and how they don't mix? It's true, especially when the oil is very hot. If you need to wash your hands when frying (which is likely, because they'll get floury), dry them thoroughly, and don't let water or other liquids splash into the oil, or it will spatter and possibly cause burns.

This should go without saying, but we'll say it: Be careful. Don't fry around children, and don't fry while you have other things on your mind or a lot going on in your house. Frying requires your full attention. Do not leave the kitchen.

Frying Doughnut Holes

Fry doughnut holes the same way you fry doughnuts, cooking them for about 75 percent of the recommended time for the doughnuts and removing them with a slotted spoon. You may notice that doughnut holes tend to roll around in the oil by themselves; you'll need to watch them to make sure they cook on all sides.

The riskiest part of frying doughnuts is actually frying the holes, whose round shapes cause the oil to squirt up right at eye level. For safety, place the holes on a metal slotted spoon or mesh strainer, and gently lower them into the oil. If you must use your hands, deposit them into the oil thin side first, like putting a coin into a machine, because they'll splash less that way.

Disposing of Oil

When used doughnut-frying oil is cool, strain it, pour it into a sealable container, and then take it to a nearby restaurant that accepts used oil, or call your local waste management company for tips. (We send our oil to a company that recycles it into biofuel.) You can also save cooled, strained oil in the refrigerator for reuse for up to two weeks.

An icing is a thick, almost spreadable doughnut topper that sits on top of the doughnut. It is always applied after doughnuts have cooled.

A glaze is a thin coating, applied when the doughnut is hot, that completely covers all of a doughnut's cracks and crevices.

Here are some tips for working with those two sweet coatings. In addition to the icings and glazes provided with the doughnut recipes, a separate chapter at the end of the book gives recipes, as well as topping ideas, that you can use to create your own doughnut combinations.

The Golden Rule of Icing and Glazing

For glazing, work while the doughnuts are hot and the glaze is warm; for icing, the doughnuts should be completely cool but the icing still warm. Note that small batches of our icings and glazes will cover a dozen doughnuts only if used at the appropriate temperature.

Using Agar

At Top Pot, all our icings and glazes use powdered agar, a stabilizer derived from seaweed that makes the icing firm up so that the doughnuts are much less fragile. It also prevents the weeping that can occur when the moisture of the doughnut seeps into the icing. (You can find online sources for agar on page 141.) For our own icing, we make a syrup using the agar, which melts into water to form a clear, slightly viscous mixture. But because the agar sets up almost immediately when it cools, we have to keep the icing warm while we use it. We use giant steam tables for this; at home, you can rewarm your icing before using it by setting it over a pan filled with 1 in/2.5 cm of barely simmering water, stirring frequently until the icing can be stirred easily.

If you're a science type, it might be useful to know that agar firms up at approximately 88°F/35°C, but once it has set, it does not melt below 136°F/85°C—so you'll have to get it good and hot to melt it once it's firm.

Making Icings and Glazes Ahead of Time

If you're making a simple icing or glaze (one without agar) ahead of time, cover the surface directly with plastic wrap/cling film until ready to use, and stir vigorously before using. You can make them while you make the doughnut dough, but it's best to use them the same day they're made. Reheating them, per the instructions above, always makes application easier.

Do not make icings or glazes with agar ahead of time.

Coloring

Icings and glazes can be tinted any color; simply add a drop or two of food coloring while mixing. Remember, you can always add more color, but it's hard to take it out.

Dipping

Top Pot's bakers apply glazes and icings by dropping a doughnut into the bowl of glaze or icing from about 6 in/15 cm above the surface—this coats just the right portion of the doughnut—then removing it with their hands, allowing a bit of the excess to drip back into the bowl. They then transfer the doughnut immediately to a cooling rack, and allow the glaze or icing to run down the sides of the doughnut naturally.

Flavoring

Icings and glazes are an excellent outlet for kitchen creativity. They can be flavored with virtually any extract, but start sparingly—some flavors go a long way. Be careful when adding more than a few drops of any liquid, because the mixture of liquid and confectioners'/icing sugar is a delicate balance in both icings and glazes.

Thinning or Thickening

If your icing or glaze seems too thick, try stirring it—it should loosen as you continue stirring. If it still seems too thick, you can thin it with a tiny amount of water. Add only a teaspoon at a time, because a small amount of liquid goes a long way.

For icings or glazes that are too thin, add additional confectioners'/icing sugar, being sure to sift it first.

If your icing has thickened because it's cooled (not because it was too thick in the first place), you can also rewarm it in a microwave-safe bowl for 15 seconds or so, to reliquefy it.

Do the Twist

If you don't feel that your doughnuts are being nicely coated in icing, try gently twisting them while they're half submerged. If that doesn't work, try rewarming or thinning as above.

TOPPINGS

Because icings and glazes dry quickly (even without agar), add toppings immediately after coating each doughnut. Do not wait until you've dipped all the doughnuts to start adding toppings.

THE TOP POT DOUGHNUTS YOU MIGHT NOT HAVE TASTED

The doughnuts in this book are our customers' favorites, and some we've always wanted to sell or have sold in the past. Of course, there are many more combinations—and since being creative is an essential part of our process, it should be part of yours, too. Experiment with abandon; you can still call them homemade Top Pot doughnuts.

Make your own glaze or icing flavors by substituting other liquids for the water or milk in our recipes, or flavor doughnuts with anything very small that won't affect the texture of the dough too much. Here are a few suggestions:

- Simple orange, apple, or cranberry glaze (made with juice instead of water) for yeast-raised doughnuts

- Ginger, cardamom, or cinnamon cake doughnuts, made with spice in the dough and icing

- Espresso doughnuts, made with instant espresso in the dough and coffee in the icing

- Double vanilla cake doughnuts, made by simmering all liquids first with a halved, scraped vanilla bean, then cooling

- Fruit-filled Bavarian cream bismarks, made by infusing cream with fruit flavorings and topping with fruit-flavored icings, instead of chocolate icing

Are there doughnuts that haven't worked for us? Sure, but we take the good with the bad. There are also a few fun flavors we've loved but decided not to sell to the public. Here are some we (or our bakers) have made:

Çar Bomb Bavarian: Like our Bavarian Cream Bismark (page 77), only topped with a Guinness chocolate icing and filled with a whiskey-spiked pastry cream.

Cherry Blossom: Each spring, for a limited time, we make Cherry Blossom doughnuts, which are Michael's favorite. They're vanilla cake doughnuts, speckled with cherry chips and topped with a cherry-infused icing.

Cristal Doughnut: Our classic raised ring, topped with a ginger ale–based glaze and finely ground Pop Rocks, for an effervescent experience.

Peanut Butter and Jelly: Our classic vanilla cake doughnut studded with peanut butter chips that ooze when you bite into them, filled with berry jam and topped with a peanut butter icing.

SPICE CAKE
DOUGHNUTS

The first doughnut Top Pot made, in 2002, was a basic spice cake doughnut, heady with nutmeg. We still love them plain, but you can also glaze or ice them, or try one of the time-tested combinations that follow. If you want to cover them in granulated or confectioners'/icing sugar, cinnamon sugar, cocoa, or plain sugar, see the instructions for sandy toppings on page 139.

BASIC SPICE CAKE DOUGHNUTS

MAKES ONE DOZEN doughnuts and holes

TOSS THESE IN SUGAR OR CINNAMON SUGAR WHEN THEY'RE STILL PIPING HOT, OR COOL THEM, then transfer them to a small paper bag filled with a few cups of powdered/icing sugar and coat them a few at a time. Glaze them when still warm, but make sure they're cool before applying any icings.

2¾ cups/315 g cake/soft-wheat flour, plus more for rolling and cutting	⅔ cup/130 g sugar	**TIME** 1 hour active time, plus glazing or icing
1 tsp baking powder	2 tbsp shortening/vegetable lard, trans-fat-free preferred	
1 tsp iodized salt	1 large egg plus 1 large egg yolk	**EQUIPMENT** Doughnut cutter (or 2¾ in/7 cm and 1¼ in/3 cm round cutters)
¾ tsp ground nutmeg	⅔ cup/165 ml whole milk	
	Canola oil, for frying	

➤ Sift the flour, baking powder, salt, and nutmeg together into a medium bowl, and set aside.

➤ In a stand mixer fitted with the paddle attachment, mix the sugar and shortening/vegetable lard for 1 minute on low speed, until sandy. Add the egg and egg yolk, then mix for 1 more minute on medium speed, scraping the sides of the bowl with a rubber spatula if necessary, until the mixture is light colored and thick.

➤ Add the dry ingredients to the wet ingredients in three separate additions, alternating with the milk, mixing until just combined on low speed each time. The dough will be very sticky, like very wet cookie/biscuit dough.

➤ Transfer the dough to a clean bowl and refrigerate, covered directly with plastic wrap/cling film, for 1 hour (or up to 24 hours).

➤ Using a candy thermometer to measure the temperature, heat oil (at least 2 in/5 cm deep) in a deep fryer, large pot, or high-sided frying pan over medium heat to 370°F/185°C. (See the frying tips on page 25.) Gently roll out the chilled dough on a counter or cutting board floured with about ¼ cup/30 g cake/soft-wheat flour to ½ in/12 mm thick, or about 8 in/20 cm in diameter, flouring the top of the dough and the rolling pin with another 2 tbsp flour, or as necessary to prevent sticking—this is a soft, wet dough. Cut into as many doughnuts and holes as possible, dipping the cutter into flour before each cut. Fold and gently reroll the dough to make extra holes (working with floured hands makes the dough less sticky), and cut again.

➤ Shake any excess flour off the doughnuts before carefully adding them to the hot oil a few at a time, taking care not to crowd them. Once the doughnuts float, fry for about 60 seconds per side, or until deep golden brown on both sides. Drain on paper towels/absorbent paper.

PINK FEATHER BOA
CAKE DOUGHNUTS

MAKES ONE DOZEN doughnuts and holes

IT WOULD BE EASY TO PREDICT THAT OUR PINK-TINGED, COCONUT-COVERED cake doughnut, named by an employee at Top Pot's first cafe, would be the favorite among little girls, but you'd be surprised how many grown-ups like it, too. Fashion designer Vera Wang once ordered a few dozen for a bridal show in New York.

For another variation popular in Seattle, make a Chocolate Feather Boa by substituting Simple Chocolate Icing (page 126) for the Pink Icing.

2¾ cups/315 g cake/soft-wheat flour, plus more for rolling and cutting	2 tbsp shortening/vegetable lard, trans-fat-free preferred	TIME
		1 hour active time, plus icing
1 tsp baking powder	1 large egg plus 1 large egg yolk	
1 tsp iodized salt	⅔ cup/165 ml whole milk	EQUIPMENT
¾ tsp ground nutmeg	Canola oil, for frying	Doughnut cutter (or 2¾ in/7 cm and 1¼ in/3 cm round cutters)
⅔ cup/130 g sugar	Pink Icing (page 128)	
	1 cup/90 g sweetened shredded/desiccated coconut	

➡ Sift the flour, baking powder, salt, and nutmeg together into a medium bowl, and set aside.

➡ In a stand mixer fitted with the paddle attachment, mix the sugar and shortening/vegetable lard for 1 minute on low speed, until sandy. Add the egg and egg yolk, then mix for 1 more minute on medium speed, scraping the sides of the bowl with a rubber spatula if necessary, until the mixture is light colored and thick.

➡ Add the dry ingredients to the wet ingredients in three separate additions, alternating with the milk, mixing until just combined on low speed each time. The dough will be very sticky, like very wet cookie/biscuit dough.

➡ Transfer the dough to a clean bowl and refrigerate, covered directly with plastic wrap/cling film, for 1 hour (or up to 24 hours).

➡ Using a candy thermometer to measure the temperature, heat oil (at least 2 in/5 cm deep) in a deep fryer, large pot, or high-sided frying pan over medium heat to 370°F/185°C. (See the frying tips on page 25.) Gently roll out the chilled dough on a counter or cutting board floured with about ¼ cup/30 g cake/soft-wheat flour to ½ in/12 mm

continued

SPICE CAKE DOUGHNUTS

thick, or about 8 in/20 cm in diameter, flouring the top of the dough and the rolling pin with another 2 tbsp flour, or as necessary to prevent sticking—this is a soft, wet dough. Cut into as many doughnuts and holes as possible, dipping the cutter into flour before each cut. Fold and gently reroll the dough to make extra holes (working with floured hands makes the dough less sticky), and cut again. *(Note: Because this is such a soft dough, you may find it easier to cut just a few doughnuts at a time, right before you add them to the oil, instead of cutting them all out ahead of time. Transferring them is easiest with a flat metal spatula.)*

■ Shake any excess flour off the doughnuts before carefully adding them to the hot oil a few at a time, taking care not to crowd them. Once the doughnuts float, fry for about 60 seconds per side, or until deep golden brown on both sides. (You'll know they're ready to turn the first time when you see the golden brown color creeping up from the bottom of the doughnut.) Drain on paper towels/absorbent paper.

■ When the doughnuts have cooled completely, dip one side of each into the warm Pink Icing. (See page 29 for icing tips.) Sprinkle the coconut on top immediately after icing each doughnut. Let dry on cooling racks, iced side up, until the icing is firm, about 15 minutes.

TRIPLE COCONUT
CAKE DOUGHNUTS

MAKES ONE DOZEN doughnuts and holes

MADE WITH COCONUT FLAVORING AND SHREDS OF COCONUT IN THE BATTER,
then dipped in a glaze made with creamy coconut milk, these doughnuts are for
coconut lovers. Make sure whatever you use to cut out the doughnuts is sharp,
so it cuts through the coconut.

COCONUT DOUGHNUTS

2¾ cups/315 g cake/soft-wheat flour, plus more for rolling and cutting

1 tsp baking powder

1 tsp iodized salt

¾ tsp ground nutmeg

⅔ cup/130 g sugar

2 tbsp shortening/vegetable lard, trans-fat-free preferred

1 large egg plus 1 large egg yolk

1 tsp coconut extract

⅔ cup/165 ml whole milk

½ cup/45 g sweetened shredded/desiccated coconut

Canola oil, for frying

COCONUT GLAZE

3½ cups/350 g confectioners'/icing sugar, sifted

1½ tsp light corn/golden syrup

¼ tsp iodized salt

½ tsp coconut extract

1 tsp vanilla extract

⅓ cup/75 ml coconut milk

1½ cups/135 g sweetened shredded/desiccated coconut (optional)

TIME

1 hour 5 minutes active time, plus glazing

EQUIPMENT

Doughnut cutter
(or 2¾ in/7 cm and 1¼ in/3 cm round cutters)

▬► First, make the doughnut dough: Sift the flour, baking powder, salt, and nutmeg together into a medium bowl, and set aside.

▬► In a stand mixer fitted with the paddle attachment, mix the sugar and shortening/vegetable lard for 1 minute on low speed, until sandy. Add the egg and egg yolk, then mix for 1 more minute on

medium speed, scraping the sides of the bowl with a rubber spatula if necessary, until the mixture is light colored and thick. Mix in the coconut extract.

▬► Add the dry ingredients to the wet ingredients in three separate additions, alternating with the milk, mixing until just combined on low speed each time and adding the shredded/desiccated coconut with the last of the flour. The dough will be very sticky, like very wet cookie/biscuit dough.

→ Transfer the dough to a clean bowl and refrigerate, covered directly with plastic wrap/cling film, for 1 hour (or up to 24 hours).

→ Meanwhile, make the glaze: Place the confectioners'/icing sugar, corn/golden syrup, salt, coconut extract, and vanilla in the work bowl of a stand mixer fitted with the paddle attachment. With the machine on medium speed, add the coconut milk in a slow, steady stream, and blend until all of the sugar has been incorporated, scraping the bowl a few times if necessary. Set aside.

→ Using a candy thermometer to measure the temperature, heat oil (at least 2 in/5 cm deep) in a deep fryer, large pot, or high-sided frying pan over medium heat to 370°F/185°C. (See the frying tips on page 25.) Gently roll out the chilled dough on a counter or cutting board floured with about ¼ cup/30 g cake/soft-wheat flour to ½ in/12 mm thick, or about 8 in/20 cm in diameter, flouring the top of the dough and the rolling pin with another 2 tbsp flour, or as necessary to prevent sticking this is a soft, wet dough. Cut into as many

doughnuts and holes as possible, dipping the cutter into flour before each cut. Fold and gently reroll the dough to make extra holes (working with floured hands makes the dough less sticky), and cut again. *(Note: Because this is such a soft dough, you may find it easier to cut just a few doughnuts at a time, right before you add them to the oil, instead of cutting them all out ahead of time. Transferring them is easiest with a flat metal spatula.)*

→ Shake any excess flour off the doughnuts before carefully adding them to the hot oil a few at a time, taking care not to crowd them. Once the doughnuts float, fry for about 60 seconds per side, or until deep golden brown on both sides. (You'll know they're ready to turn the first time when you see the golden brown color creeping up from the bottom of the doughnut.) Drain on paper towels/absorbent paper.

→ While the doughnuts are still quite hot, dip one side of each into the warm Coconut Glaze. (See page 29 for glazing tips.) If topping with coconut, sprinkle it on immediately after glazing each doughnut. Let dry on cooling racks, glazed side up, for about 15 minutes.

VALLEY GIRL LEMON DOUGHNUTS

MAKES ONE DOZEN doughnuts and holes

TOP POT SERVES VALLEY GIRL LEMON DOUGHNUTS, WHICH GET THEIR NAME from plenty of spunky, sassy flavor, two different ways: as a lemon-spiked cake doughnut with puckery lemon icing, as in this recipe, and as a lemon bismark filled with lemon curd.

If you're a fan of combining lemon flavor with poppy seeds, stir ¼ cup/30 g poppy seeds into the dry ingredients, and sprinkle additional seeds over the top, immediately after icing each doughnut.

LEMON DOUGHNUTS

3 cups/355 g cake/soft-wheat flour, plus more for rolling and cutting

1 tsp baking powder

1 tsp iodized salt

⅔ cup/130 g sugar

2 tbsp shortening/vegetable lard, trans-fat-free preferred

1 large egg plus 1 large egg yolk

1 tsp vanilla extract

½ tsp lemon extract

Grated zest of 1 large lemon

2 tsp freshly squeezed lemon juice

⅔ cup/165 ml whole milk

Canola oil, for frying

LEMON ICING

4½ cups/1 lb box/450 g confectioners'/icing sugar, sifted

1½ tsp light corn/golden syrup

¼ tsp iodized salt

½ tsp vanilla extract

Grated zest of 1 large lemon

1 drop yellow food coloring (optional)

3 tbsp freshly squeezed lemon juice

2 tbsp hot water

TIME

1 hour 10 minutes active time, plus icing

EQUIPMENT

Doughnut cutter
(or 2¾ in/7 cm and 1¼ in/3 cm round cutters)

First, make the doughnut dough: Sift the flour, baking powder, and salt together into a medium bowl, and set aside.

In a stand mixer fitted with the paddle attachment, mix the sugar and shortening/vegetable lard for 1 minute on low speed, until sandy. Add the egg and egg yolk, then mix for 1 more minute on medium speed, scraping the sides of the bowl with a rubber spatula if necessary, until the mixture is light colored and thick. Mix in the vanilla and lemon extracts, lemon zest, and lemon juice.

Add the dry ingredients to the wet ingredients in three separate additions, alternating with the milk, mixing until just combined on low speed each time. The dough will be very sticky, like very wet cookie/biscuit dough.

➡ Transfer the dough to a clean bowl and refrigerate, covered directly with plastic wrap/cling film, for 1 hour (or up to 24 hours).

➡ Meanwhile, make the icing: Place the confectioners'/icing sugar, corn/golden syrup, salt, vanilla, lemon zest, and food coloring in the work bowl of a stand mixer fitted with the paddle attachment. With the machine on medium speed, add the lemon juice and water in a slow, steady stream, and blend until all of the sugar has been incorporated, scraping the bowl a few times if necessary. Set aside.

➡ Using a candy thermometer to measure the temperature, heat oil (at least 2 in/5 cm deep) in a deep fryer, large pot, or high-sided frying pan over medium heat to 370°F/185°C. (See the frying tips on page 25.) Gently roll out the chilled dough on a counter or cutting board floured with about ¼ cup/30 g cake/soft-wheat flour to ½ in/12 mm thick, or about 8 in/20 cm in diameter, flouring the top of the dough and the rolling pin with another 2 tbsp flour, or as necessary to prevent sticking—

this is a soft, wet dough. Cut into as many doughnuts and holes as possible, dipping the cutter into flour before each cut. Fold and gently reroll the dough to make extra holes (working with floured hands makes the dough less sticky), and cut again. *(Note: Because this is such a soft dough, you may find it easier to cut just a few doughnuts at a time, right before you add them to the oil, instead of cutting them all out ahead of time. Transferring them is easiest with a flat metal spatula.)*

➡ Shake any excess flour off the doughnuts before carefully adding them to the hot oil a few at a time, taking care not to crowd them. Once the doughnuts float, fry for about 60 seconds per side, or until deep golden brown on both sides. (You'll know they're ready to turn the first time when you see the golden brown color creeping up from the bottom of the doughnut.) Drain on paper towels/absorbent paper.

➡ When the doughnuts have cooled completely, dip one side of each into the warm Lemon Icing. (See page 29 for icing tips.) Let dry on cooling racks, iced side up, until the icing is firm, about 15 minutes.

BLUEBERRY CAKE DOUGHNUTS

MAKES ONE DOZEN doughnuts and holes

STUFFED WITH BLUEBERRIES AND TOPPED WITH A GLAZE TINTED WITH BLUEBERRY jam, these are a surefire way to convince a die-hard chocolate lover that doughnuts with fruit in them are worth eating. Any berry (fresh or frozen) will work, but smaller blueberries make the dough easier to handle. If you're using frozen berries, increase the flour to 3 cups/355 g.

2¾ cups/315 g cake/soft-wheat flour, plus more for rolling and cutting

1 tsp baking powder

1 tsp iodized salt

¼ tsp ground nutmeg

⅔ cup/130 g sugar

2 tbsp shortening/vegetable lard, trans-fat-free preferred

1 large egg plus 1 large egg yolk

⅔ cup/165 ml whole milk

¾ cup/110 g blueberries

Canola oil, for frying

Berry Glaze (page 134), made with blueberry jam

TIME

1 hour active time, plus glazing

EQUIPMENT

Doughnut cutter
(or 2¾ in/7 cm and 1¼ in/3 cm round cutters)

➡ Sift the flour, baking powder, salt, and nutmeg together into a medium bowl, and set aside.

➡ In a stand mixer fitted with the paddle attachment, mix the sugar and shortening/vegetable lard for 1 minute on low speed, until sandy. Add the egg and egg yolk, then mix 1 more minute on medium speed, scraping the sides of the bowl with a spatula if necessary, until the mixture is light and thick.

➡ Add the dry ingredients to the wet ingredients in three separate additions, alternating with the milk, mixing until just combined on low speed each time. Mix in the blueberries. The dough will be very sticky, like very wet cookie/biscuit dough.

➡ Transfer the dough to a clean bowl and refrigerate, covered directly with plastic wrap/cling film, for 1 hour (or up to 24 hours).

➡ Using a candy thermometer to measure the temperature, heat oil (at least 2 in/5 cm deep) in a deep fryer, large pot, or high-sided frying pan over medium heat to 370°F/185°C. (See the frying tips on page 25.) Gently roll out the chilled dough on a counter or cutting board floured with about ¼ cup/30 g cake/soft-wheat flour to ½ in/12mm thick, or about 8 in/20 cm in diameter, flouring the top of the dough and the rolling pin with another 2 tbsp flour, or as necessary to prevent sticking—

SPICE CAKE DOUGHNUTS

continued

this is a soft, wet dough. Cut into as many dough-nuts and holes as possible, dipping the cutter into flour before each cut. Fold and gently reroll the dough to make extra holes (working with floured hands makes the dough less sticky), and cut again. *(Note: Because this is such a soft dough, you may find it easier to cut the doughnuts just a few at a time, right before you add them to the oil, instead of cutting them all out ahead of time. Transferring them is easiest with a flat metal spatula.)*

➤ Shake any excess flour off the doughnuts before carefully adding them to the hot oil a few at a time, taking care not to crowd them. Once the doughnuts float, fry for about 60 seconds per side, or until deep golden brown on both sides. (You'll know they're ready to turn the first time when you see the golden brown color creeping up from the bottom of the doughnut.) Drain on paper towels/ absorbent paper.

➤ While the doughnuts are still quite hot, dip one side into the warm Berry Glaze. (See page 29 for glazing tips.) Let dry on cooling racks, glazed side up, for about 15 minutes.

ORANGE-PISTACHIO CAKE DOUGHNUTS

MAKES ONE DOZEN doughnuts and holes

BY SUBSTITUTING DIFFERENT EXTRACTS AND NUTS, YOU CAN GET A HUGE
variety of flavors out of this classic combo. Try using lime extract, zest, and juice
in the doughnuts and icing, along with coconut extract, and top with macadamia nuts,
or replace the orange and pistachio with lemon and almond flavors.

Ingredients		Time & Equipment
3 cups/355 g cake/soft-wheat flour, plus more for rolling and cutting	1 tsp vanilla extract	TIME
1 tsp baking powder	Grated zest of 1 large orange	1 hour 5 minutes active time, plus icing
1 tsp iodized salt	½ tsp orange extract	
⅔ cup/130 g sugar	⅔ cup/165 ml whole milk	EQUIPMENT
2 tbsp shortening/vegetable lard, trans-fat-free preferred	Canola oil, for frying	Doughnut cutter (or 2¾ in/7 cm and 1¼ in/3 cm round cutters)
1 large egg plus 1 large egg yolk	Triple Orange Icing (page 130)	
	1 cup/125 g finely chopped pistachio nuts	

Sift the flour, baking powder, and salt together into a medium bowl, and set aside.

In a stand mixer fitted with the paddle attachment, mix the sugar and shortening/vegetable lard for 1 minute on low speed, until sandy. Add the egg and egg yolk, then mix for 1 more minute on medium speed, scraping the sides of the bowl with a rubber spatula if necessary, until the mixture is light colored and thick. Stir in the vanilla, orange zest, and orange extract.

Add the dry ingredients to the wet ingredients in three separate additions, alternating with the milk, mixing until just combined on low speed each time. The dough will be very sticky, like very wet cookie/biscuit dough.

Transfer the dough to a clean bowl and refrigerate, covered directly with plastic wrap/cling film, for 1 hour (or up to 24 hours).

Using a candy thermometer to measure the temperature, heat oil (at least 2 in/5 cm deep) in a deep fryer, large pot, or high-sided frying pan over medium heat to 370°F/185°C. (See the frying tips on page 25.) Gently roll out the chilled dough on a counter or cutting board floured with about ¼ cup/30 g cake/soft-wheat flour to ½ in/12 mm thick, or about 8 in/20 cm in diameter, flouring the top of the dough and the rolling pin with another 2 tbsp flour, or as necessary to prevent sticking—this is a soft, wet dough. Cut into as many doughnuts and holes as possible, dipping the cutter into

SPICE CAKE DOUGHNUTS

continued

flour before each cut. Fold and gently reroll the dough to make extra holes (working with floured hands makes the dough less sticky), and cut again. *(Note: Because this is such a soft dough, you may find it easier to cut just a few doughnuts at a time, right before you add them to the oil, instead of cutting them all out ahead of time. Transferring them is easiest with a flat metal spatula.)*

➤ Shake any excess flour off the doughnuts before carefully adding them to the hot oil a few at a time, taking care not to crowd them. Once the doughnuts float, fry for about 60 seconds per side, or until deep golden brown on both sides. (You'll know they're ready to turn the first time when you see the golden brown color creeping up from the bottom of the doughnut.) Drain on paper towels/ absorbent paper.

➤ When the doughnuts have cooled completely, dip one side of each into the warm Triple Orange Icing. (See page 29 for icing tips.) Sprinkle with the pistachios immediately after icing each doughnut. Let dry on cooling racks, iced side up, until the icing is firm, about 15 minutes.

SPICED CHAI
CAKE DOUGHNUTS

MAKES ONE DOZEN doughnuts and holes

MADE WITH A COMBINATION OF NUTMEG, CINNAMON, GINGER, CLOVES,
and cardamom, these sweetly spiced doughnuts, which we first made for Starbucks,
are our dessert version of chai tea.

SPICED CHAI DOUGHNUTS

2¾ cups/315 g cake/soft-wheat flour,
plus more for rolling and cutting

1 tsp baking powder

1 tsp iodized salt

¾ tsp ground nutmeg

¾ tsp ground ginger

¼ tsp ground cloves

½ tsp ground cinnamon

¾ tsp ground cardamom

⅔ cup/130 g sugar

2 tbsp shortening/vegetable lard,
trans-fat-free preferred

1 large egg plus 1 large egg yolk

⅔ cup/165 ml whole milk

Canola oil, for frying

SPICED CHAI ICING

4½ cups/1 lb/450 g confectioners'/
icing sugar, sifted

1½ tsp light corn/golden syrup

¼ tsp iodized salt

1 tsp vanilla extract

⅓ cup/75 ml prepared sweetened
hot chai tea (such as Oregon Chai)

TIME

1 hour 5 minutes active time,
plus icing

EQUIPMENT

Doughnut cutter
(or 2¾ in/7 cm and 1¼ in/3 cm
round cutters)

➥ First, make the doughnut dough: Sift the flour, baking powder, salt, and spices together into a medium bowl, and set aside.

➥ In a stand mixer fitted with the paddle attachment, mix the sugar and shortening/vegetable lard for 1 minute on low speed, until sandy. Add the egg and egg yolk, then mix for 1 more minute on medium speed, scraping the sides of the bowl with a rubber spatula if necessary, until the mixture is light colored and thick.

➥ Add the dry ingredients to the wet ingredients in three separate additions, alternating with the milk, mixing until just combined on low speed each time. The dough will be very sticky, like very wet cookie/biscuit dough.

➥ Transfer the dough to a clean bowl and refrigerate, covered directly with plastic wrap/cling film, for 1 hour (or up to 24 hours).

➥ Meanwhile, make the icing: Place the confectioners'/icing sugar, corn/golden syrup, salt, and vanilla in the work bowl of a stand mixer fitted with the paddle attachment. With the machine on medium speed, add the tea in a slow, steady stream, and blend until all of the sugar has been incorporated, scraping the bowl a few times, if necessary. Set aside.

➡ Using a candy thermometer to measure the temperature, heat oil (at least 2 in/5 cm deep) in a deep fryer, large pot, or high-sided frying pan over medium heat to 370°F/185°C. (See the frying tips on page 25.) Gently roll out the chilled dough on a counter or cutting board floured with about ¼ cup/30 g cake/soft-wheat flour to ½ in/12 mm thick, or about 8 in/20 cm in diameter, flouring the top of the dough and the rolling pin with another 2 tbsp flour, or as necessary to prevent sticking—this is a soft, wet dough. Cut into as many doughnuts and holes as possible, dipping the cutter into flour before each cut. Fold and gently reroll the dough to make extra holes (working with floured hands makes the dough less sticky), and cut again. *(Note: Because this is such a soft dough, you may find it easier to cut just a few doughnuts at a time, right before you add them to the oil, instead of cutting them all out ahead of time. Transferring them is easiest with a flat metal spatula.)*

➡ Shake any excess flour off the doughnuts before carefully adding them to the hot oil a few at a time, taking care not to crowd them. Once the doughnuts float, fry for about 60 seconds per side, or until deep golden brown on both sides. (You'll know they're ready to turn the first time when you see the golden brown color creeping up from the bottom of the doughnut.) Drain on paper towels/absorbent paper.

➡ When the doughnuts have cooled completely, dip one side of each into the warm Spiced Chai Icing. (See page 29 for icing tips.) Let dry on cooling racks, iced side up, until the icing is firm, about 15 minutes.

A WISH!

e candles

DEVIL'S FOOD CAKE
DOUGHNUTS

Made with Dutch-processed cocoa powder for a
light dough that has plenty of chocolate flavor,
our chocolate cake doughnuts are infinitely
toppable. Start with the basics—the Double
Trouble is a chocolate lover's dream—but don't
miss some of our more creative versions, like
the Chocolate-Chili Cake Doughnuts and the
Dulce de Leche Cake Doughnuts.

BASIC DEVIL'S FOOD CAKE DOUGHNUTS

MAKES ONE DOZEN doughnuts and holes

THERE'S NO AFTERNOON SNACK QUITE AS SATISFYING AS A CHOCOLATE cake doughnut—unless, of course, it's a chocolate cake doughnut coated in sugar or your favorite icing. Make this basic version, or try one of the classic (or not-so-classic) variations that follow. Although any unsweetened cocoa powder will work, Dutch-processed cocoa has a richer flavor that we think makes a tastier doughnut.

See page 138 for topping ideas.

2 cups/225 g cake/soft-wheat flour, plus more for rolling and cutting	½ cup/100 g sugar	**TIME**
½ cup/50 g unsweetened Dutch-processed cocoa powder	2 tbsp shortening/vegetable lard, trans-fat-free preferred	1 hour active time, plus glazing or icing
1 tsp baking powder	2 large egg yolks	**EQUIPMENT**
1 tsp iodized salt	1 tsp vanilla extract	Doughnut cutter (or 2¾ in/7 cm and 1¼ in/3 cm round cutters)
¾ tsp ground nutmeg	⅔ cup/165 ml whole milk	
	Canola oil, for frying	

➡ Sift the flour, cocoa powder, baking powder, salt, and nutmeg together into a medium bowl, and set aside.

➡ In a stand mixer fitted with the paddle attachment, mix the sugar and shortening/vegetable lard for 1 minute on low speed, until sandy. Add the egg yolks one at a time, then mix for 1 more minute on medium speed, scraping the sides of the bowl with a rubber spatula if necessary, until the mixture is light colored and thick. Mix in the vanilla.

➡ Add the dry ingredients to the wet ingredients in three separate additions, alternating with the milk, mixing until just combined on low speed each time. The dough will be sticky, like cookie/biscuit dough.

➡ Transfer the dough to a clean bowl and refrigerate, covered with plastic wrap/cling film, for 45 minutes (or up to 24 hours).

➡ Using a candy thermometer to measure the temperature, heat oil (at least 2 in/5 cm deep) in a deep fryer, large pot, or high-sided frying pan over medium heat to 370°F/185°C. (For frying tips, see page 25.) Roll out the chilled dough on a counter or cutting board sprinkled with 2 to 3 tbsp flour to ½ in/12 mm thick, or about 8 in/20 cm in diameter, flouring the top of the dough and the rolling pin as necessary to prevent sticking. Cut into as many doughnuts and holes as possible, dipping the cutter into flour before each cut. Fold and gently reroll the dough to make extra holes (working with floured hands makes the dough less sticky), and cut again.

➤ Shake any excess flour off the doughnuts before carefully adding them to the hot oil a few at a time, taking care not to crowd them. Once the doughnuts float, fry for about 60 seconds per side—you won't be able to see when the doughnuts brown because of the chocolate, but you'll see a change in texture. Drain on paper towels/absorbent paper.

DOUBLE TROUBLE CAKE DOUGHNUTS

MAKES ONE DOZEN doughnuts and holes

TOP POT SELLS THESE CHOCOLATE-FROSTED CHOCOLATE DOUGHNUTS
straight up, but feel free to top them with even more chocolate—sprinkles/sugar strands,
mini chocolate chips, small chocolate candies, or anything else you can dream up.

2 cups/225 g cake/soft-wheat flour,
plus more for rolling and cutting

½ cup/50 g unsweetened Dutch-
processed cocoa powder

1 tsp baking powder

1 tsp iodized salt

¾ tsp ground nutmeg

½ cup/100 g sugar

2 tbsp shortening/vegetable lard,
trans-fat-free preferred

2 large egg yolks

1 tsp vanilla extract

⅔ cup/165 ml whole milk

Canola oil, for frying

Simple Chocolate Icing (page 126)
or Top Pot's Chocolate Doughnut
Icing (page 125)

TIME
1 hour active time,
plus icing

EQUIPMENT
Doughnut cutter
(or 2¾ in/7 cm and 1¼ in/3 cm
round cutters)

➡ Sift the flour, cocoa powder, baking powder, salt, and nutmeg together into a medium bowl, and set aside.

➡ In a stand mixer fitted with the paddle attachment, mix the sugar and shortening/vegetable lard for 1 minute on low speed, until sandy. Add the egg yolks one at a time, then mix for 1 more minute on medium speed, scraping the sides of the bowl with a rubber spatula if necessary, until the mixture is light colored and thick. Mix in the vanilla.

➡ Add the dry ingredients to the wet ingredients in three separate additions, alternating with the milk, mixing until just combined on low speed each time. The dough will be sticky, like cookie/biscuit dough.

➡ Transfer the dough to a clean bowl and refrigerate, covered with plastic wrap/cling film, for 45 minutes (or up to 24 hours).

➡ Using a candy thermometer to measure the temperature, heat oil (at least 2 in/5 cm deep) in a deep fryer, large pot, or high-sided frying pan over medium heat to 370°F/185°C. (For frying tips, see page 25.) Roll out the chilled dough on a counter or cutting board sprinkled with 2 to 3 tbsp flour to ½ in/12 mm thick, or about 8 in/20 cm in diameter, flouring the top of the dough and the rolling pin as necessary to prevent sticking. Cut into as many doughnuts and holes as possible, dipping the cutter into flour before each cut. Fold and gently reroll the dough to make extra holes (working with floured hands makes the dough less sticky), and cut again.

➡ Shake any excess flour off the doughnuts before carefully adding them to the hot oil a few at a time, taking care not to crowd them. Once the doughnuts float, fry for about 60 seconds per side—you won't be able to see when the doughnuts brown because of the chocolate, but you'll see a change in texture. Drain on paper towels/absorbent paper.

➡ When the doughnuts have cooled completely, dip one side of each into the warm chocolate icing. (See page 29 for icing tips.) Sprinkle on any decorations immediately after icing each doughnut. Let dry on cooling racks, iced side up, until the icing is firm, 10 to 15 minutes.

CHOCOLATE-ORANGE CAKE DOUGHNUTS

MAKES ONE DOZEN doughnuts and holes

THE COMBINATION OF CHOCOLATE AND ORANGE, LIKE THOSE FOIL-WRAPPED chocolate oranges sold around the holidays, is a classic. If you're looking for Halloween treats, tint the Triple Orange Icing with one drop each of red and yellow food coloring and top the doughnuts with chocolate sprinkles/sugar strands.

2 cups/225 g cake/soft-wheat flour, plus more for rolling and cutting

½ cup/50 g unsweetened Dutch-processed cocoa powder

1 tsp baking powder

1 tsp iodized salt

¾ tsp ground nutmeg

½ cup/100 g sugar

2 tbsp shortening/vegetable lard, trans-fat-free preferred

2 large egg yolks

1 tsp vanilla extract

½ tsp orange extract

Grated zest of 1 large orange

⅔ cup/165 ml whole milk

Canola oil, for frying

Triple Orange Icing (page130)

TIME
1 hour 5 minutes active time, plus icing

EQUIPMENT
Doughnut cutter
(or 2¾ in/7 cm and 1¼ in/3 cm round cutters)

➡ Sift the flour, cocoa powder, baking powder, salt, and nutmeg together into a medium bowl, and set aside.

➡ In a stand mixer fitted with the paddle attachment, mix the sugar and shortening/vegetable lard for 1 minute on low speed, until sandy. Add the egg yolks one at a time, then mix for 1 more minute on medium speed, scraping the sides of the bowl with a rubber spatula if necessary, until the mixture is light colored and thick. Mix in the vanilla and orange extracts, and orange zest.

➡ Add the dry ingredients to the wet ingredients in three separate additions, alternating with the milk, mixing until just combined on low speed each time. The dough will be sticky, like cookie/biscuit dough.

➡ Transfer the dough to a clean bowl and refrigerate, covered with plastic wrap/cling film, for 45 minutes (or up to 24 hours).

➡ Using a candy thermometer to measure the temperature, heat oil (at least 2 in/5 cm deep) in a deep fryer, large pot, or high-sided frying pan over medium heat to 370°F/185°C. (For frying tips, see page 25.) Roll out the chilled dough on a counter or cutting board sprinkled with 2 to 3 tbsp flour to ½ in/12 mm thick, or about 8 in/20 cm in diameter, flouring the top of the dough and the rolling pin as necessary to prevent sticking. Cut into as many doughnuts and holes as possible, dipping the cutter into flour before each cut. Fold and gently reroll the dough to make extra holes (working with floured hands makes the dough less sticky), and cut again.

➡ Shake any excess flour off the doughnuts before carefully adding them to the hot oil a few at a time, taking care not to crowd them. Once the doughnuts float, fry for about 60 seconds per side—you won't be able to see when the doughnuts brown because of the chocolate, but you'll see a change in texture. Drain on paper towels/absorbent paper.

➡ When the doughnuts have cooled completely, dip one side of each into the warm Triple Orange Icing. (See page 29 for icing tips.) Sprinkle on any decorations immediately after icing each doughnut. Let dry on cooling racks, iced side up, until the icing is firm, 10 to 15 minutes.

PEPPERMINT SNOWDRIFT
CAKE DOUGHNUTS

MAKES ONE DOZEN doughnuts and holes

WHEN WE RELEASED THIS DOUGHNUT AFTER OPENING OUR FIFTH AVENUE STORE
in Seattle, we topped a minty version of our signature chocolate cake doughnuts with a drift
of white peppermint icing and shards of peppermint candies and called them Peppermint
Avalanches—but something about that name didn't sit well with us. We prefer
Peppermint Snowdrifts, and now we top them with festive red sanding sugar.
Add the decorations immediately after icing each doughnut, or they won't stick.

CHOCOLATE PEPPERMINT DOUGHNUTS	PEPPERMINT ICING	TIME
2 cups/225 g cake/soft-wheat flour, plus more for rolling and cutting	4½ cups/1 lb/450 g confectioners'/ icing sugar, sifted	1 hour active time, plus icing
½ cup/50 g unsweetened Dutch-processed cocoa powder	1½ tsp light corn/golden syrup	EQUIPMENT
1 tsp baking powder	¼ tsp iodized salt	Doughnut cutter (or 2¾ in/7 cm and 1¼ in/3 cm round cutters)
1 tsp iodized salt	½ tsp vanilla extract	
¾ tsp ground nutmeg	¼ tsp peppermint extract	
½ cup/100 g sugar	⅓ cup/75 ml plus 1 tbsp hot water	
2 tbsp shortening/vegetable lard, trans-fat-free preferred	Red sanding sugar or peppermint candy shards, for decoration	
2 large egg yolks		
1 tsp vanilla extract		
½ tsp peppermint extract		
⅔ cup/165 ml whole milk		
Canola oil, for frying		

➡ First, make the doughnut dough: Sift the flour, cocoa powder, baking powder, salt, and nutmeg together into a mixing bowl, and set aside.

➡ In a stand mixer fitted with the paddle attachment, mix the sugar and shortening/vegetable lard for 1 minute on low speed, until sandy. Add the egg

continued

yolks one at a time, then mix for 1 more minute on medium speed, scraping the sides of the bowl with a rubber spatula if necessary, until the mixture is light colored and thick. Mix in the vanilla and peppermint extracts.

➧ Add the dry ingredients to the wet ingredients in three separate additions, alternating with the milk, mixing until just combined on low speed each time. The dough will be sticky, like cookie/biscuit dough.

➧ Transfer the dough to a clean bowl and refrigerate, covered with plastic wrap/cling film, for 45 minutes (or up to 24 hours).

➧ Meanwhile, make the icing: Place the confectioners'/icing sugar, corn/golden syrup, salt, vanilla, and peppermint extract in the work bowl of a stand mixer fitted with the paddle attachment. With the machine on medium speed, add the water in a slow, steady stream, and blend until all of the sugar has been incorporated, scraping the bowl a few times if necessary. Set aside.

➧ Using a candy thermometer to measure the temperature, heat oil (at least 2 in/5 cm deep) in a deep fryer, large pot, or high-sided frying pan over medium heat to 370°F/185°C. (For frying tips see page 25.) Roll out chilled dough on a counter or cutting board sprinkled with 2 to 3 tbsp flour to $1/2$ in/12mm thick, or about 8 in/20 cm in diameter, flouring the top of the dough and the rolling pin as necessary to prevent sticking. Cut into as many doughnuts and holes as possible, dipping the cutter into flour before each cut. Fold and gently reroll the dough to make extra holes (working with floured hands makes the dough less sticky), and cut again.

➧ Shake any excess flour off the doughnuts before carefully adding them to the hot oil a few at a time, taking care not to crowd them. Once the doughnuts float, fry for about 60 seconds per side. You won't be able to see when the doughnuts brown because of the chocolate, but you'll see a change in texture.

➧ When the doughnuts have cooled completely, dip one side of each into the warm icing. (See page 29 for icing tips.) Sprinkle on the decorations immediately after icing each doughnut. Let dry on cooling racks, iced side up, for 10 to 15 minutes.

MAPLE-ICED CHOCOLATE CAKE DOUGHNUTS

MAKES ONE DOZEN doughnuts and holes

IF YOU'RE LOOKING TO SATISFY TWO CRAVINGS AT ONCE,
try topping a rich chocolate cake doughnut with maple icing.
For extra intrigue, top with chopped walnuts and crisp bacon bits.

2 cups/225 g cake/soft-wheat flour, plus more for rolling and cutting	2 tbsp shortening/vegetable lard, trans-fat-free preferred	TIME 1 hour active time, plus icing
½ cup/50 g unsweetened Dutch processed cocoa powder	2 large egg yolks	EQUIPMENT Doughnut cutter (or 2¾ in/7 cm and 1¼ in/3 cm round cutters)
1 tsp baking powder	1 tsp vanilla extract	
1 tsp iodized salt	⅔ cup/165 ml whole milk	
¾ tsp ground nutmeg	Canola oil, for frying	
½ cup/100 g sugar	Maple Icing (page 128)	

Sift the flour, cocoa powder, baking powder, salt, and nutmeg together into a medium bowl, and set aside.

In a stand mixer fitted with the paddle attachment, mix the sugar and shortening/vegetable lard for 1 minute on low speed, until sandy. Add the egg yolks one at a time, then mix for 1 more minute on medium speed, scraping the sides of the bowl with a rubber spatula if necessary, until the mixture is light colored and thick. Mix in the vanilla.

Add the dry ingredients to the wet ingredients in three separate additions, alternating with the milk, mixing until just combined on low speed each time. The dough will be sticky, like cookie/biscuit dough.

Transfer the dough to a clean bowl and refrigerate, covered with plastic wrap/cling film, for 45 minutes (or up to 24 hours).

Using a candy thermometer to measure the temperature, heat oil (at least 2 in/5 cm deep) in a deep fryer, large pot, or high-sided frying pan over medium heat to 370°F/185°C. (For frying tips, see page 25.) Roll out the chilled dough on a counter or cutting board sprinkled with 2 to 3 tbsp flour to ½ in/12 mm thick, or about 8 in/20 cm in diameter, flouring the top of the dough and the rolling pin as necessary to prevent sticking. Cut into as many doughnuts and holes as possible, dipping the cutter into flour before each cut. Fold and gently reroll the dough to make extra holes (working with floured hands makes the dough less sticky), and cut again.

continued

DEVIL'S FOOD CAKE DOUGHNUTS

i'm fried

➤ Shake any excess flour off the doughnuts before carefully adding them to the hot oil a few at a time, taking care not to crowd them. Once the doughnuts float, fry for about 60 seconds per side—you won't be able to see when the doughnuts brown because of the chocolate, but you'll see a change in texture. Drain on paper towels/absorbent paper.

➤ When the doughnuts have cooled completely, dip one side of each into the warm Maple Icing. (See page 29 for icing tips.) Sprinkle on any decorations immediately after icing each doughnut. Let dry on cooling racks, iced side up, for 10 to 15 minutes.

CHOCOLATE SAND CASTLES CAKE DOUGHNUTS

MAKES ONE DOZEN doughnuts and holes

IT WOULD BE NICE, WE THINK, IF A DAY AT THE BEACH MEANT COMING HOME coated in a strong cinnamon sugar, like these chocolate cake doughnuts, instead of actual sand. To make the cinnamon sugar stick, be sure to toss the doughnuts in the sugar while they're still good and hot.

CHOCOLATE DOUGHNUTS

2 cups/225 g cake/soft-wheat flour, plus more for rolling and cutting

½ cup/50 g unsweetened Dutch-processed cocoa powder

1 tsp baking powder

1 tsp iodized salt

¾ tsp ground nutmeg

½ cup/100 g sugar

2 tbsp shortening/vegetable lard, trans-fat-free preferred

2 large egg yolks

1 tsp vanilla extract

⅔ cup/165 ml whole milk

Canola oil, for frying

TOPPING

1½ cups/300 g sugar

1 tbsp ground cinnamon

TIME

1 hour 10 minutes active time

EQUIPMENT

Doughnut cutter
(or 2¾ in/7 cm and 1¼ in/3 cm round cutters)

➡ First, make the doughnut dough: Sift the flour, cocoa powder, baking powder, salt, and nutmeg together into a medium bowl, and set aside.

➡ In a stand mixer fitted with the paddle attachment, mix the sugar and shortening/vegetable lard for 1 minute on low speed, until sandy. Add the egg yolks one at a time, then mix for 1 more minute on medium speed, scraping the sides of the bowl with a rubber spatula if necessary, until the mixture is light colored and thick. Mix in the vanilla.

➡ Add the dry ingredients to the wet ingredients in three separate additions, alternating with the milk, mixing until just combined on low speed each time. The dough will be sticky, like cookie/biscuit dough.

➡ Transfer the dough to a clean bowl and refrigerate, covered with plastic wrap/cling film, for 45 minutes (or up to 24 hours).

➡ Make the topping: Mix the sugar and cinnamon together in a large bowl and set aside.

➡ Using a candy thermometer to measure the temperature, heat oil (at least 2 in/5 cm deep) in a deep fryer, large pot, or high-sided frying pan over medium heat to 370°F/185°C. (For frying tips see page 25.) Roll out chilled dough on a counter or cutting board sprinkled with 2 to 3 tbsp flour to ½ in/12mm thick, or about 8 in/20 cm in diameter, flouring the top of the dough and the rolling pin as necessary to prevent sticking—this is a soft, wet dough. Cut into as many doughnuts and holes as possible, dipping the cutter into flour before each cut. Fold and gently reroll the dough to make extra holes (working with floured hands makes the dough less sticky), and cut again.

➡ Shake any excess flour off the doughnuts before carefully adding them to the hot oil a few at a time, taking care not to crowd them. Once

the doughnuts float, fry for about 60 seconds per side—you won't be able to see when the doughnuts brown because of the chocolate, but you'll see a change in texture. Drain briefly on paper towels/absorbent paper.

➡ As soon as you can touch the doughnuts comfortably, toss them in the cinnamon sugar, coating them on all sides. Eat warm.

DEVIL'S FOOD CAKE DOUGHNUTS

CHOCOLATE-CHILI CAKE DOUGHNUTS

MAKES ONE DOZEN doughnuts and holes

MADE WITH CHOCOLATE, CHILI, CINNAMON, AND PEANUTS, THESE MOLE-INSPIRED doughnuts are a departure from our classics. Adjust the amount of chili powder according to your taste preferences—but note that these doughnuts are less spicy when they've cooled than they are when still a bit warm, so spice them according to when you'll eat them. Sweet, spicy, and salty, they're delicious with a glass of horchata.

CHOCOLATE-CHILI DOUGHNUTS

2 cups/225 g cake/soft-wheat flour, plus more for rolling and cutting

½ cup/50 g unsweetened Dutch-processed cocoa powder

1 tsp baking powder

1 tsp iodized salt

½ tsp ground nutmeg

½ tsp ground cinnamon

2 tsp chili powder

½ cup/100 g sugar

2 tbsp shortening/vegetable lard, trans-fat-free preferred

2 large egg yolks

⅔ cup/165 ml whole milk

Canola oil, for frying

CHOCOLATE-CHILI ICING

3½ cups/350 g confectioners'/icing sugar, sifted

2 tbsp unsweetened Dutch-processed cocoa powder, sifted

1½ tsp light corn/golden syrup

¼ tsp iodized salt

1 tsp chili powder, plus more if desired

½ tsp ground cinnamon

⅓ cup/75 ml hot water

1½ cups/200 g finely chopped salted peanuts

TIME

1 hour 10 minutes active time, plus icing

EQUIPMENT

Doughnut cutter (or 2¾ in/7 cm and 1¼ in/3 cm round cutters)

➡ First, make the doughnut dough: Sift the flour, cocoa powder, baking powder, salt, nutmeg, cinnamon, and chili powder together into a medium bowl, and set aside.

➡ In a stand mixer fitted with the paddle attachment, mix the sugar and shortening/vegetable lard for 1 minute on low speed, until sandy. Add the egg yolks one at a time, then mix for 1 more minute on medium speed, scraping the sides of the bowl with a rubber spatula if necessary, until the mixture is light colored and thick.

➥ Add the dry ingredients to the wet ingredients in three separate additions, alternating with the milk, mixing until just combined on low speed each time. The dough will be sticky, like cookie/biscuit dough.

➥ Transfer the dough to a clean bowl and refrigerate, covered with plastic wrap/cling film, for 45 minutes (or up to 24 hours).

➥ Meanwhile, make the icing: Place the confectioners'/icing sugar, cocoa powder, corn/golden syrup, salt, chili powder, and cinnamon in the work bowl of a stand mixer fitted with the paddle attachment. With the machine on medium speed, add the water in a slow, steady stream, and blend until all of the sugar has been incorporated, scraping the bowl a few times if necessary. Taste the icing. If you'd like more spice, add chili powder, 1/2 tsp at a time, mixing between additions, until you've reached the desired spice level. Set aside.

➥ Using a candy thermometer to measure the temperature, heat oil (at least 2 in/5 cm deep) in a deep fryer, large pot, or high-sided frying pan over medium heat to 370°F/185°C. (For frying tips, see page 25.) Roll out the chilled dough on a counter or cutting board sprinkled with 2 to 3 tbsp flour to 1/2 in/12 mm thick, or about 8 in/20 cm in diameter, flouring the top of the dough and the rolling pin as necessary to prevent sticking. Cut into as many doughnuts and holes as possible, dipping the cutter into flour before each cut. Fold and gently reroll the dough to make extra holes (working with floured hands makes the dough less sticky), and cut again.

➥ Shake any excess flour off the doughnuts before carefully adding them to the hot oil a few at a time, taking care not to crowd them. Once the doughnuts float, fry for about 60 seconds per side—you won't be able to see when the doughnuts brown because of the chocolate, but you'll see a change in texture. Drain on paper towels/absorbent paper.

➥ When the doughnuts have cooled completely, dip one side of each into the warm icing. (See page 29 for icing tips.) Sprinkle the peanuts on immediately after glazing each doughnut. Let dry on cooling racks, peanut side up, for 10 to 15 minutes.

DULCE DE LECHE CAKE DOUGHNUTS

MAKES ONE DOZEN doughnuts and holes

OUR VERSION OF DULCE DE LECHE INCLUDES CHOCOLATE—SPECIFICALLY, a chocolate cake doughnut spotted with caramel bits (or butterscotch chips) that stay gooey for a few hours, topped with a rich chocolate caramel icing. For this recipe, a real doughnut cutter is a plus, because the edges are sharp enough to get through the caramel bits.

DULCE DE LECHE DOUGHNUTS

2 cups/225 g cake/soft-wheat flour, plus more for rolling and cutting

½ cup/50 g unsweetened Dutch-processed cocoa powder

1 tsp baking powder

1 tsp iodized salt

¾ tsp ground nutmeg

½ cup/100 g sugar

2 tbsp shortening/vegetable lard, trans-fat-free preferred

2 large egg yolks

1 tsp vanilla extract

⅔ cup/165 ml whole milk

¾ cup/180 g caramel bits or butterscotch chips

Canola oil, for frying

DULCE DE LECHE ICING BASE

4½ cups/1 lb/450 g confectioners'/icing sugar, sifted

2 tbsp unsweetened Dutch-processed cocoa powder, sifted

1½ tsp light corn/golden syrup

¼ tsp iodized salt

¼ tsp vanilla extract

⅓ cup/75 ml plus 1 tbsp hot water, plus more if needed

CARAMEL

½ cup/100 g sugar

¼ cup/60 ml water

¼ cup/60 ml heavy (whipping)/double cream

TIME

1 hour 20 minutes active time, plus icing

EQUIPMENT

Doughnut cutter (or 2¾ in/7 cm and 1¼ in/3 cm round cutters)

▶ First, make the doughnut dough: Sift the flour, cocoa powder, baking powder, salt, and nutmeg together into a medium bowl, and set aside.

▶ In a stand mixer fitted with the paddle attachment, mix the sugar and shortening/vegetable lard for 1 minute on low speed, until sandy. Add the egg

yolks one at a time, then mix for 1 more minute on medium speed, scraping the sides of the bowl with a rubber spatula if necessary, until the mixture is light colored and thick. Mix in the vanilla.

▶ Add the dry ingredients to the wet ingredients in three separate additions, alternating with the milk, mixing until just combined on low speed each time and adding the caramel bits with the last of the flour. The dough will be sticky, like cookie/biscuit dough.

➤ Transfer the dough to a clean bowl and refrigerate, covered with plastic wrap/cling film, for 45 minutes (or up to 24 hours).

➤ While the dough chills, make the icing base: Place the confectioners'/icing sugar, cocoa powder, corn/golden syrup, salt, vanilla, and hot water in a large mixing bowl or in the work bowl of a stand mixer fitted with the paddle attachment. Using a whisk, or with the machine on low speed, blend until the mixture is smooth and all of the sugar has been incorporated, scraping the sides of the bowl with a rubber spatula if necessary.

➤ Next, make the caramel: Combine the sugar and water in a small, nonreactive saucepan over high heat. Stir until the sugar dissolves, then cook at a high simmer, undisturbed, swirling the pan (but not stirring) occasionally, until the caramel turns an amber color, 6 to 8 minutes. Remove from the heat. While whisking (or swirling the pan by its handle), very carefully add the cream in a slow, steady stream, and continue whisking until the caramel stops bubbling. Let cool for 10 minutes.

➤ Add the warm caramel to the icing base, and stir to blend. If the icing seems too thick, add more hot water, a teaspoonful at a time. Set aside.

➤ Using a candy thermometer to measure the temperature, heat oil (at least 2 in/5 cm deep) in a deep fryer, large pot, or high-sided frying pan over medium heat to 370°F/185°C. (For frying tips, see page 25. You may want to start heating the oil while you make the caramel.) Roll out the chilled dough on a counter or cutting board sprinkled with 2 to 3 tbsp flour to ½ in/12 mm thick, or about 8 in/20 cm in diameter, flouring the top of the dough and the rolling pin as necessary to prevent sticking. Cut into as many doughnuts and holes as possible, dipping the cutter into flour before each cut. Fold and gently reroll the dough to make extra holes (working with floured hands makes the dough less sticky) and cut again.

➤ Shake any excess flour off the doughnuts before carefully adding them to the hot oil a few at a time, taking care not to crowd them. Once the doughnuts float, fry for about 60 seconds per side—you won't be able to see when the doughnuts brown because of the chocolate, but you'll see a change in texture. Drain on paper towels/absorbent paper.

➤ When the doughnuts have cooled completely, dip one side of each into the warm icing. (See page 29 for icing tips.) Dry on cooling racks, iced side up, for 10 to 15 minutes.

RAISED
DOUGHNUTS

Although yeast-raised doughnuts require a bit of a time commitment, because the dough rises twice, either rise can take place overnight. To refrigerate unformed, just-made dough, place it in a large, oiled bowl, lightly oil the top, cover the bowl (not just the dough) with plastic wrap/cling film, refrigerate, and roll the dough out in the morning. (The residual heat of the dough will make it rise while you're sleeping.) You can also complete the first rise, form the doughnuts, transfer them to floured baking sheets/trays, and refrigerate them, well wrapped in plastic/film, overnight. Give them a second rise as directed in the morning.

RAISED GLAZED RING
DOUGHNUTS

MAKES 1 DOZEN, more if rerolled (plus holes)

AT TOP POT, THE RAISED GLAZED DOUGHNUTS ARE CUT WITH A REGULAR
doughnut cutter, then stretched and left to rise in our giant proofing oven for
an eye-popping final size. At home, it's easier to make them slightly smaller,
so you can fry more than one or two at a time. Look for mace, which is the spice
made from the outer layer of a nutmeg seed, in your grocery store's spice aisle.

Since the glaze works best while the doughnuts are still very warm,
make the glaze while the doughnuts are rising the second time.

---

3 tbsp (four ¼ oz/7 g packets)
active dry yeast

1 cup/240 ml very warm water
(about 105°F/40°C)

½ cup/100 g sugar, plus 1 tbsp

½ tsp baking powder

½ tsp ground mace

2 tsp iodized salt

4 to 4½ cups/550 to 620 g bread/
strong flour, plus more for rolling
and cutting

¼ cup/55 g shortening/vegetable
lard, trans-fat-free preferred

3 large egg yolks

½ tsp vanilla extract

Canola oil, for frying

Small batch Simplest Vanilla Glaze
(page 132) or Top Pot's Vanilla
Doughnut Glaze (page 131)

TIME
1 hour active time,
plus glazing

EQUIPMENT
Doughnut cutter
(or 2¾ in/7 cm and 1¼ in/3 cm
round cutters)

Whisk the yeast, water, and 1 tbsp of the sugar together in the work bowl of a stand mixer and set aside for 5 minutes.

In a large bowl, whisk together the remaining ½ cup/100 g sugar, baking powder, mace, salt, and 4 cups/550 g of the bread/strong flour. Set aside.

Add the shortening/vegetable lard, egg yolks, and vanilla to the foaming yeast mixture. Mix with the paddle attachment on low speed for 1 minute, to break up the shortening. Add about a third of the dry ingredients and mix until blended on low speed, then repeat with the second third of the dry ingredients.

Switch to the dough hook and add the remaining dry ingredients, mixing on low speed until no white spots remain each time, adding additional flour as necessary, until the dough is dry enough to clean the bottom of the bowl. Increase the speed to medium and knead for 2 more minutes. (It should be smooth like bread dough, but still a bit tacky.)

➡ Transfer the dough to a baking sheet/tray sprinkled with 1 tbsp flour, shape into a flat disk 6 in/15 cm in diameter, dust lightly with flour, cover with a dish/tea towel, and set aside.

➡ Create a proofing box in your oven: Bring a large kettle of water to a boil. Pour 8 cups/2 L of the boiling water into a 9-by-13-in/25-by-35-cm (or similar) baking dish, and set it on the floor of your oven. Place the sheet/tray with the covered dough on the middle rack of the oven, close the door, and let the dough rise until doubled in size, about 1 hour. (For tips on making your dough ahead of time, see page 71.)

➡ Transfer the dough to a lightly floured work surface and roll into a roughly 12 in/30 cm circle, about ½ in/12 mm thick, with a lightly floured rolling pin. Cut into 12 doughnuts, flouring the cutter before each cut. (Reroll the dough for additional doughnuts.) Gently transfer the doughnuts (and holes) to two baking sheets/trays sprinkled with 2 tbsp flour

each, arranging them at least 2 in/5 cm apart, and let rise in the oven (with new boiling water), uncovered, for another 30 to 45 minutes, until doubled in size.

➡ Using a candy thermometer to measure the temperature, heat oil (at least 2 in/5 cm deep) in a deep fryer, large pot, or high-sided frying pan over medium heat to 350°F/180°C. (For frying tips, see page 25.) When the doughnuts have doubled, carefully place a few in the oil, taking care not to overcrowd them, and fry for about 30 seconds. (Note that the doughnuts will look more brown when they're done than they do in the oil.) Carefully turn the doughnuts and fry for another 20 to 30 seconds, until golden on the second side, then transfer to a cooling rack set over a layer of paper towels/absorbent paper to cool, rounded side up.

➡ While the doughnuts are still very warm, dip the rounded side of each into the warm glaze. (See page 29 for glazing tips.) Let dry on cooling racks, glazed side up, for 10 to 15 minutes.

Tip: Use any dough scraps to make Classic Twists (page 75) or Apple Fritters (page 88).

CLASSIC TWISTS

MAKES ONE DOZEN large twists

THE TOP POT CAFES IN SEATTLE, WASHINGTON, NO LONGER MAKE THESE TWISTS,
but you may recognize them from airports across America that sell Top Pot Doughnuts.
Because the twists have lots of surface area, it's easiest to glaze them when
they're still very hot, so the glaze spreads easily. Use our Simplest Vanilla Glaze (page 132)
if you're working alone, so you can make it ahead and have it ready when the twists
come out of the fryer, or have a helper make Top Pot's Vanilla Doughnut Glaze (page 131)
while you're frying the first batch. These doughnuts are rather large, so you'll need a frying
vessel that can accommodate a twist up to 8 in/20 cm long.

Note: You can make Classic Twists using scraps left over from other recipes.
Divide the dough into balls that fit easily in the palm of your hand (about 3 oz/85 g each),
and use the twisting instructions that follow.

---

3 tbsp (four ¼ oz/7 g packets) active dry yeast	¼ cup/55 g shortening/vegetable lard, trans-fat-free preferred	TIME
1 cup/240 ml very warm water (about 105°F/40°C)	3 large egg yolks	1 hour 5 minutes active time, plus glazing
½ cup/100 g sugar, plus 1 tbsp	½ tsp vanilla extract	EQUIPMENT
½ tsp baking powder	Canola oil, for frying	Pizza cutter
½ tsp ground mace	Big batch Simplest Vanilla Glaze (page 132) or Top Pot's Vanilla Doughnut Glaze (page 131)	
2 tsp iodized salt		
4 to 4½ cups/550 to 620 g bread/ strong flour, plus more for rolling and cutting		

Whisk the yeast, water, and 1 tbsp of the sugar together in the work bowl of a stand mixer and set aside for 5 minutes.

In a large bowl, whisk together the remaining ½ cup/100 g sugar, baking powder, mace, salt, and 4 cups/550 g of the bread/strong flour. Set aside.

continued

Add the shortening/vegetable lard, egg yolks, and vanilla to the foaming yeast mixture. Mix with the paddle attachment on low speed for 1 minute, to break up the shortening. Add about a third of the dry ingredients and mix until blended on low speed, then repeat with the second third of the dry ingredients.

Switch to the dough hook and add the remaining dry ingredients, mixing on low speed until no white spots remain each time, adding additional flour as necessary, until the dough is dry enough to clean the bottom of the bowl. Increase the speed to medium and knead for 2 more minutes. (It should be smooth like bread dough, but still a bit tacky.)

Transfer the dough to a baking sheet/tray sprinkled with 1 tbsp flour, shape into a flat square 6 in/15 cm across, dust lightly with flour, cover with a dish/tea towel, and set aside.

Create a proofing box in your oven: Bring a large kettle of water to a boil. Pour 8 cups/2 L of the boiling water into a 9-by-13-in/25-by-35-cm (or similar) baking dish, and set it on the floor of your oven. Place the sheet with the covered dough on the middle rack of the oven, close the door, and let the dough rise until doubled in size, about 1 hour. (For tips on making your dough ahead of time, see page 71.)

Transfer the dough to a lightly floured work surface and roll or press into a roughly 10 in/25 cm square. Using a pizza cutter or a large, sharp knife, cut the dough into 12 strips of equal width. Working with one piece at a time on an unfloured surface, roll the dough into 12 "snakes," each about 18 in/45 cm long and $1/2$ in/12 mm in diameter, allowing the dough to rest, if necessary, if it begins to spring back as you work with it. Let the dough snakes rest for 5 minutes. Holding one end of a snake in each hand, twist it 5 or 6 times, so it begins to coil up and look like a rope. Fold the rope in thirds, twist the tripled rope 3 or 4 times, and pinch the ends together. Repeat with the remaining snakes, gently transferring the folded twists to two lightly floured baking sheets/trays, arranging them at least 2 in/5 cm apart. Let rise in the oven (with new boiling water), uncovered, for another 30 to 45 minutes, until doubled in size.

Using a candy thermometer to measure the temperature, heat oil (at least 2 in/5 cm deep) in a deep fryer, large pot, or high-sided frying pan over medium heat to 350°F/180°C. (For frying tips, see page 25.) When the twists have doubled, carefully place one or two in the oil, taking care not to overcrowd them, and fry for about 30 to 40 seconds, or until light golden brown on the bottom. (Note that the twists will look more brown when they're done than they do in the oil.) Carefully turn the twists and fry for another 20 to 30 seconds, until golden on the second side, then transfer to a cooling rack set over a layer of paper towels/absorbent paper to cool, rounded side up.

While the twists are still very warm, dip the most rounded side of each into the warm glaze. (See page 29 for glazing tips.) Let dry on cooling racks, glazed side up, for 10 to 15 minutes.

BAVARIAN CREAM BISMARKS

MAKES ONE DOZEN large doughnuts

ALSO CALLED BOSTON CREAMS, OUR CUSTARD-STUFFED, CHOCOLATE-ICED doughnuts are a giant treat. Make the cream filling first (up to 3 days ahead), because it needs to chill completely before you fill the doughnuts. Since the icing works best when the doughnuts are cool but the icing is still warm, make the icing after you've fried the doughnuts.

CREAM FILLING

8 large egg yolks

⅔ cup/130 g sugar

2 tsp vanilla extract

¼ tsp iodized salt

½ cup/60 g plus 1 tbsp all-purpose/plain flour

2½ cups/600 ml half-and-half/half cream, warmed

DOUGHNUTS

3 tbsp (four ¼ oz/7 g packets) active dry yeast

1 cup/240 ml very warm water (about 105°F/40°C)

½ cup/100 g sugar, plus 1 tbsp

½ tsp baking powder

½ tsp ground mace

2 tsp iodized salt

4 to 4½ cups/550 to 620 g bread/strong flour, plus more for rolling and cutting

¼ cup/55 g shortening/vegetable lard, trans-fat-free preferred

3 large egg yolks

½ tsp vanilla extract

Canola oil, for frying

Simple Chocolate Icing (page 128) or Top Pot's Chocolate Doughnut Icing (page 125)

TIME

1 hour 20 minutes active time, plus icing and filling

EQUIPMENT

3 in/7.5 cm pastry cutter, clean tin can, or jelly jar; pastry/piping bag with plain ½ in/1 cm tip

➡ First, make the cream filling: Whisk the egg yolks and sugar in a small saucepan until thick and one shade lighter in color. Add the vanilla, salt, and flour, and whisk until no white spots remain. Whisk in the warm half-and-half/half cream, then place the saucepan over medium heat and cook, stirring constantly, until the mixture thickens and begins to bubble, 8 to 10 minutes. (As it cooks, the cream may begin to get lumpy on the bottom of the pan—use a rubber spatula to scrape it off as it cooks, then use a whisk to break up any lumps.) When the mixture has bubbled a few times and is the consistency of sour cream, transfer it to a mixing bowl. Cover the surface of the filling directly with plastic wrap/cling film, and poke the wrap/film with a knife to allow steam to escape. Let cool to room temperature, then refrigerate until chilled through, at least 4 hours.

continued

RAISED DOUGHNUTS

Make the doughnut dough: Whisk the yeast, water, and 1 tbsp of the sugar together in the work bowl of a stand mixer and set aside for 5 minutes.

In a large bowl, whisk together the remaining ½ cup/100 g sugar, baking powder, mace, salt, and 4 cups/550 g of the bread/strong flour. Set aside.

Add the shortening/vegetable lard, egg yolks, and vanilla to the foaming yeast mixture. Mix with the paddle attachment on low speed for 1 minute, to break up the shortening. Add about a third of the dry ingredients and mix until blended on low speed, then repeat with the second third of the dry ingredients.

Switch to the dough hook and add the remaining dry ingredients, mixing on low speed until no white spots remain each time, adding additional flour as necessary, until the dough is dry enough to clean the bottom of the bowl. Increase the speed to medium and knead for 2 more minutes. (It should be smooth like bread dough, but still a bit tacky.)

Transfer the dough to a baking sheet/tray sprinkled with 1 tbsp flour, shape into a flat disk 6 in/15 cm in diameter, dust lightly with flour, cover with a dish/tea towel, and set aside.

Create a proofing box in your oven: Bring a large kettle of water to a boil. Pour 8 cups/2 L of the boiling water into a 9-by-13-in/25-by-35-cm (or similar) baking dish, and set it on the floor of your oven. Place the sheet/tray with the covered dough on the middle rack of the oven, close the door, and let the dough rise until doubled in size, about 1 hour. (For tips on making your dough ahead of time, see page 71.)

Transfer the dough to a lightly floured work surface and roll into a roughly 12 in/30 cm circle, about ½ in/12 mm thick, with a lightly floured rolling pin. Cut into 12 rounds, flouring the cutter before each cut. (Reroll the dough for additional doughnuts.) Gently transfer the doughnuts to two baking sheets/trays sprinkled with 2 tbsp flour each, arranging them at least 2 in/5 cm apart, and let rise in the oven (with new boiling water), uncovered, for another 30 to 45 minutes, until doubled in size.

Using a candy thermometer to measure the temperature, heat oil (at least 2 in/5 cm deep) in a deep fryer, large pot, or high-sided frying pan over medium heat to 350°F/180°C. (For frying tips, see page 25.) When the doughnuts have doubled, carefully place a few in the oil, taking care not to overcrowd them, and fry for about 30 seconds, or until light golden brown on the bottom. (Note that the doughnuts will look more brown when they're done than they do in the oil.) Carefully turn the doughnuts and fry for another 20 to 30 seconds, until golden on the second side, then transfer to a cooling rack set over a layer of paper towels/absorbent paper to cool, rounded side up.

While the doughnuts cool a bit, fill a pastry/piping bag fitted with a plain tip (although any tip will work) with about a quarter of the cream filling. When the doughnuts are still a little warm, poke the pastry/piping tip into the side of a doughnut, and add pastry cream until the doughnut feels heavy—stop if you feel the seams or the bottom of the doughnut cracking open. Use this portion of filling to fill three doughnuts, then repeat with the remaining filling and doughnuts.

⬛ When all of the doughnuts have been filled carefully, dip one side of each into the warm chocolate icing. (See page 29 for icing tips.) Let dry on cooling racks, iced side up, for 10 to 15 minutes.

LEAVING YOUR MARK

After their second rise, yeast-raised doughnuts are a picture of poofy perfection. But when your rings or bars are ready for the hot oil, be careful—one bad move from you could result in a very wonky doughnut. When you transfer the doughnuts to the oil, don't grab them by the sides with your hands, because your fingers will leave big indentations that will stick around when frying. Instead, use a bench scraper, thin plastic cutting board, or large flat spatula to pick up the doughnut up with one hand. Transfer the doughnut into the other hand, so that the side that was on the baking sheet/tray is now against the palm of your hand, and slide it into the oil from there. Avoiding touching the doughnut's sticky top will ensure prettier doughnuts, too.

RASPBERRY BULLSEYES

MAKES ONE DOZEN (plus belly buttons)

ACCORDING TO JAIME TARPINIAN, ONE OF TOP POT'S BAKERS, THE BEST DOUGHNUT is the one no one ever has a chance to buy—and it's only one bite. To make bullseyes—glazed raised doughnuts filled with jam in the center—the dough is cut with a regular doughnut cutter, but the hole, or "belly button," is left in while the dough rises and cooks. After glazing, the glazed centers are easily removed to make neat little holes for the jam, leaving the lucky doughnut maker with one fresh, perfect bite. Choose a jam that has an even texture and is thick enough to hold up in an ice cream scoop.

3 tbsp (four ¼ oz/7 g packages) active dry yeast

1 cup/240 ml very warm water (about 105°F/40°C)

½ cup/100 g sugar, plus 1 tbsp

½ tsp baking powder

½ tsp ground mace

2 tsp iodized salt

4 to 4½ cups/550 to 620 g bread/strong flour, plus more for rolling and cutting

¼ cup/55 g shortening/vegetable lard, trans-fat-free preferred

3 large egg yolks

½ tsp vanilla extract

Canola oil, for frying

Big batch Simplest Vanilla Glaze (page 132) or Top Pot's Vanilla Doughnut Glaze (page 131)

1 cup/240 g thick raspberry jam

TIME

1 hour 5 minutes active time, plus glazing and filling

EQUIPMENT

Doughnut cutter (or 2¾ in/7 cm and 1¼ in/3 cm round cutters)

Whisk the yeast, water, and 1 tbsp of the sugar together in the work bowl of a stand mixer and set aside for 5 minutes.

In a large bowl, whisk together the remaining ½ cup/100 g sugar, baking powder, mace, salt, and 4 cups/550 g of the bread/strong flour. Set aside.

Add the shortening/vegetable lard, egg yolks, and vanilla to the foaming yeast mixture. Mix with the paddle attachment on low speed for 1 minute,

to break up the shortening. Add about a third of the dry ingredients and mix until blended on low speed, then repeat with the second third of the dry ingredients.

Switch to the dough hook and add the remaining dry ingredients, mixing on low speed until no white spots remain each time, adding additional flour as necessary, until the dough is dry enough to clean the bottom of the bowl. Increase the speed

continued

to medium and knead for 2 more minutes. (It should be smooth like bread dough, but still a bit tacky.)

➡ Transfer the dough to a baking sheet/tray sprinkled with 1 tbsp flour, shape into a flat disc 6 in/15 cm in diameter, dust lightly with flour, cover with a dish/tea towel, and set aside.

➡ Create a proofing box in your oven: Bring a large kettle of water to a boil. Pour 8 cups/2 L of the boiling water into a 9-by-13-in/25-by-35-cm (or similar) baking dish, and set it on the floor of your oven. Place the sheet/tray with the covered dough on the middle rack of the oven, close the door, and let the dough rise until doubled in size, about 1 hour. (For tips on making your dough ahead of time, see page 71.)

➡ Transfer the dough to a lightly floured work surface and roll into a roughly 12 in/30 cm circle, about 1/2 in/12 mm thick, with a lightly floured rolling pin. Cut into 12 rounds, flouring the cutter before each cut, using the big cutter for the outside ring and the small cutter for the inside ring if you don't have a doughnut cutter. (Reroll the dough for additional doughnuts.) Gently transfer the doughnuts, *keeping the holes intact or placing them back into the centers of the doughnuts,* to two baking sheets/trays sprinkled with 2 tbsp flour each, arranging them at least 2 in/5 cm apart, and let rise in the oven (with new boiling water), uncovered, for another 30 to 45 minutes, until doubled in size.

➡ Using a candy thermometer to measure the temperature, heat oil (at least 2 in/5 cm deep) in a deep fryer, large pot, or high-sided frying pan over medium heat to 350°F/180°C. (For frying tips, see page 25.) When the doughnuts have doubled, carefully place a few in the oil, taking care not to overcrowd them or drop the holes out, and fry for about 30 seconds, or until light golden brown on the bottom. (Note that the doughnuts will look more brown when they're done than they do in the oil.) Carefully turn the doughnuts and fry another 20 to 30 seconds, until golden on the second side, then transfer to a cooling rack set over a layer of paper towels/absorbent paper to cool, belly button side up.

➡ While the doughnuts are still very warm, dip the most rounded side of each into the warm glaze. Let dry on cooling racks, glazed side up, for 10 to 15 minutes. (See page 29 for glazing tips.) Pull out the belly buttons. Fill each hole with 1 tbsp of raspberry jam (we find that a tiny ice cream scoop works well here) and serve.

MAPLE BARS

MAKES ONE DOZEN large rolls

AT SEATTLE'S QWEST FIELD, HOME TO THE SEATTLE SEAHAWKS,
Top Pot sells close to 1,000 doughnuts each game. Half of those are maple bars,
the classic monster yeast-raised bars slathered with maple icing. Since the
icing works best when the doughnuts are cool but the icing is still warm,
make the icing after you've fried the doughnuts.

3 tbsp (four ¼ oz/7 g packages)
active dry yeast

1 cup/240 ml very warm water
(about 105°F/40°C)

½ cup/100 g sugar, plus 1 tbsp

½ tsp baking powder

½ tsp ground mace

2 tsp iodized salt

4 to 4½ cups/550 to 620 g bread/
strong flour, plus more for rolling
and cutting

¼ cup/55 g shortening/vegetable
lard, trans-fat-free preferred

3 large egg yolks

½ tsp vanilla extract

Canola oil, for frying

Maple Icing (page 128)

TIME
55 minutes active time,
plus icing

EQUIPMENT
Pizza cutter

➡ Whisk the yeast, water, and 1 tbsp of the sugar together in the work bowl of a stand mixer and set aside for 5 minutes.

➡ In a large bowl, whisk together the remaining ½ cup/100 g sugar, baking powder, mace, salt, and 4 cups/550 g of the bread/strong flour. Set aside.

➡ Add the shortening/vegetable lard, egg yolks, and vanilla to the foaming yeast mixture. Mix with the paddle attachment on low speed for 1 minute, to break up the shortening. Add about a third of the dry ingredients and mix until blended on low speed, then repeat with the second third of the dry ingredients.

➡ Switch to the dough hook and add the remaining dry ingredients, mixing on low speed until no white spots remain each time, adding additional flour as necessary, until the dough is dry enough to clean the bottom of the bowl. Increase the speed to medium and knead for 2 more minutes. (It should be smooth like bread dough, but still a bit tacky.)

➡ Transfer the dough to a baking sheet/tray sprinkled with 1 tbsp flour, shape into a flat square

continued

6 in/15 cm across, dust lightly with flour, cover with a dish/tea towel, and set aside.

➥ Create a proofing box in your oven: Bring a large kettle of water to a boil. Pour 8 cups/2 L of the boiling water into a 9-by-13-in/25-by-35-cm (or similar) baking dish, and set it on the floor of your oven. Place the sheet/tray with the covered dough on the middle rack of the oven, close the door, and let the dough rise until doubled in size, about 1 hour. (For tips on making your dough ahead of time, see page 71.)

➥ Transfer the dough to a lightly floured work surface and roll into an 11 in/25 cm by 12 in/30 cm rectangle. Using a pizza cutter or a large, sharp knife, trim about 1/2 in/12 mm off of each edge, then cut the dough into 12 bars, each 5 in/10 cm by 1 1/2 in/4 cm. Gently transfer the bars to two lightly floured baking sheets/trays, arranging them at least 2 in/5 cm apart, and let rise in the oven (with new boiling water), uncovered, for another 30 to 45 minutes, until doubled in size.

➥ Using a candy thermometer to measure the temperature, heat oil (at least 2 in/5 cm deep) in a deep fryer, large pot, or high-sided frying pan over medium heat to 350°F/180°C. (For frying tips, see page 25.) When the bars have doubled, carefully place one or two in the oil, taking care not to overcrowd them, and fry for about 30 to 40 seconds, or until light golden brown. (Note that the bars will look more brown when they're done than they do in the oil.) Carefully turn the bars and fry for another 20 to 30 seconds, until golden on the second side, then transfer to a cooling rack set over a layer of paper towels/absorbent paper to cool, rounded side up.

➥ Cool the bars completely. When cool, dip the most rounded side of each into the warm Maple Icing. (See page 29 for icing tips.) Let dry on cooling racks, iced side up, for 10 to 15 minutes.

Tip: To keep the bars' shape when transferring them to the oil, lift them off the sheets with a flat spatula or a rubber baking scraper. Work from the long side, because lifting them from one short end will stretch and distort their shapes.

HICKORY DICKORY DOCK

At Top Pot, we roll a docker (see page 22) over the dough to poke holes in our yeast-raised bar, bismark, and bullseye doughs before the second rise, to prevent bubbles from forming in the dough during frying. It makes for smoother, more even doughnuts, but if you're not a perfectionist, it's not necessary. If you don't have a docker but want to give it a try, use a wooden skewer to poke holes about 1 in/2.5 cm apart all over the yeast-raised doughnuts mentioned above.

PERSHINGS

MAKES ONE DOZEN large rolls

NAMED FOR GENERAL PERSHING, THE ONLY U.S. GENERAL TO BE PROMOTED
to the army's highest rank while he was still alive, pershings are, we assume,
the epitome of formed, raised doughnuts. Use a flat metal spatula to lift them off
the baking sheet, so the spirals stay intact. Slide your hand underneath the top of the
doughnut after you dip it into the glaze, to prevent it from unraveling as you take
it out —it's messy, but fingers really do work best.

ROLLS

3 tbsp (four ¼ oz/7 g packages)
active dry yeast

1 cup/240 ml very warm water
(about 105°F/40°C)

½ cup/100 g sugar, plus 1 tbsp

½ tsp baking powder

½ tsp ground mace

2 tsp iodized salt

4 to 4½ cups/550 to 620 g bread/
strong flour, plus more for rolling
and cutting

¼ cup/55 g shortening/vegetable
lard, trans-fat-free preferred

3 large egg yolks

½ tsp vanilla extract

FILLING

1 tbsp whole milk

1 large egg

½ cup/100 g sugar

1 tbsp ground cinnamon

Canola oil, for frying

Big batch Simplest Vanilla Glaze
(page 132) or Top Pot's Vanilla
Doughnut Glaze (page 131)

TIME

1 hour active time,
plus glazing

EQUIPMENT

Large, sharp knife

━ First, make the rolls: Whisk the yeast, water, and 1 tbsp of the sugar together in the work bowl of a stand mixer and set aside for 5 minutes.

━ In a large bowl, whisk together the remaining ½ cup/100 g sugar, baking powder, mace, salt, and 4 cups/550 g of the bread/strong flour. Set aside.

━ Add the shortening/vegetable lard, egg yolks, and vanilla to the foaming yeast mixture. Mix with the paddle attachment on low speed for 1 minute, to break up the shortening. Add about a third of the dry ingredients and mix until blended on low speed, then repeat with the second third of the dry ingredients.

continued

Switch to the dough hook and add the remaining dry ingredients, mixing on low speed until no white spots remain each time, adding additional flour as necessary, until the dough is dry enough to clean the bottom of the bowl. Increase the speed to medium and knead for 2 more minutes. (It should be smooth like bread dough but still a bit tacky.)

Transfer the dough to a baking sheet/tray sprinkled with 1 tbsp flour, shape into a flat square 6 in/15 cm across, dust lightly with flour, cover with a dish/tea towel, and set aside.

Create a proofing box in your oven: Bring a large kettle of water to a boil. Pour 8 cups/2 L of the boiling water into a 9-by-13-in/25-by-35-cm (or similar) baking dish, and set it on the floor of your oven. Place the sheet/tray with the covered dough on the middle rack of the oven, close the door, and let the dough rise until doubled in size, about 1 hour. (For tips on making your dough ahead of time, see page 71.)

Transfer the dough to a lightly floured cutting board and roll into a roughly 12 in/30 cm square, about 1/2 in/12 mm thick, with a lightly floured rolling pin.

To make the filling: Whisk the milk and egg together in a small bowl, and brush a layer over the entire surface of the dough. (You won't use all of the egg wash.) In another bowl, mix the sugar and cinnamon together, then sprinkle the mixture over the dough, leaving a 1 in/2.5 cm strip at one end empty. Roll up the dough into a loose log, ending

with the empty strip. (This will help the rolls stick together.) Use a large, sharp knife to cut the log into 12 slices 1 in/2.5 cm thick. Gently transfer the rolls to two baking sheets/trays sprinkled with 2 tbsp flour each, arranging them at least 2 in/5 cm apart. Fold the ends of the spirals underneath the rolls if they begin to unravel, and gently press the rolls into a round shape if they've become square. Let rise in the oven (with new boiling water), uncovered, for another 30 to 45 minutes, until doubled in size.

Using a candy thermometer to measure the temperature, heat oil (at least 2 in/5 cm deep) in a deep fryer, large pot, or high-sided frying pan over medium heat to 340°F/170°C. (For frying tips, see page 25.) When the rolls have doubled, carefully place one or two in the oil, taking care not to overcrowd them, and fry for about 30 to 40 seconds, or until light golden brown on the bottom. (Note that the doughnuts will look more brown when they're done than they do in the oil.) Carefully turn the doughnuts and fry for another 20 to 30 seconds, until golden on the second side, then transfer to a cooling rack set over a layer of paper towels/absorbent paper to cool, rounded side up.

While the pershings are still very warm, dip the most rounded side of each into the warm glaze. (See page 29 for glazing tips.) Let dry on cooling racks, glazed side up, for 10 to 15 minutes.

APPLE FRITTERS

MAKES ONE DOZEN fritters

A LOT OF WORK GOES INTO MAKING APPLE FRITTERS ON A LARGE SCALE, and watching the bakers make them at Top Pot is a full sensory experience. First, a cinnamon cloud rises up over the forming bench as the dough is layered with sweet cooked apples and huge handfuls of spice. Performed by professionals, the cutting process that combines fruit and dough reminds us of a bakery-grade jackhammer. This home-friendly version, which requires significantly less elbow grease, makes palm-size fritters, because our colossal version is simply too large to fry at home.

Note: You can make Apple Fritters using scraps left over from other recipes. This dough weighs about 1 pound/455 g. To make fritters, weigh your extra dough and adjust the recipe that follows accordingly. (If you don't want to do the math, just make the filling, spread it in a thin layer over half your extra dough, sprinkle heavily with cinnamon and flour, and proceed as directed. Serve any excess filling over ice cream!)

FRITTER DOUGH

1½ tbsp (two ¼ oz/7 g packages) active dry yeast

½ cup/120 ml very warm water (about 105°F/40°C)

¼ cup/50 g sugar, plus 2 tsp

¼ tsp baking powder

¼ tsp ground mace

1 tsp iodized salt

2 cups/275 g plus 4 to 6 tbsp bread/strong flour, plus more for rolling and cutting

2 tbsp shortening/vegetable lard, trans-fat-free preferred

1 large egg

¼ tsp vanilla extract

APPLE FILLING

2 medium tart apples, chopped into ½ in/2 cm pieces (about 2½ cups/250 g)

¼ cup/50 g sugar

2 tsp freshly squeezed lemon juice

1 tbsp plus 1 tsp ground cinnamon

1 tbsp bread/strong flour

Canola oil, for frying

Big batch Simplest Vanilla Glaze (page 132) or Top Pot's Vanilla Doughnut Glaze (page 131)

TIME

1 hour 5 minutes active time, plus glazing

EQUIPMENT

Metal bench scraper or large knife

To make the fritter dough: Whisk the yeast, water, and 2 tsp of the sugar together in the work bowl of a stand mixer and set aside for 5 minutes.

In a large bowl, whisk together the remaining ¼ cup/50 g sugar, baking powder, mace, salt, and 2 cups/275 g of the bread/strong flour. Set aside.

Add the shortening/vegetable lard, egg, and vanilla to the foaming yeast mixture. Mix with the paddle attachment on low speed for 1 minute, to break up the shortening. Add about a third of the dry ingredients and mix until blended on low speed, then repeat with the second third of the dry ingredients.

Switch to the dough hook and add the remaining dry ingredients, mixing on low speed until no white spots remain each time, adding additional flour as necessary, until the dough is dry enough to clean the bottom of the bowl. Increase the speed to medium and knead for 2 more minutes. (It should be smooth like bread dough, but still a bit tacky.)

Transfer the dough to a baking sheet/tray sprinkled with 1 tbsp flour, shape into a flat 4 in/10 cm square, dust lightly with flour, cover with a dish/tea towel, and set aside.

Create a proofing box in your oven: Bring a large kettle of water to a boil. Pour 8 cups/2 L of the boiling water into a 9-by-13-in/25-by-35-cm (or similar) baking dish, and set it on the floor of your oven. Place the sheet with the covered dough on the middle rack of the oven, close the door, and let the dough rise until doubled in size, about 1 hour. (For tips on making your dough ahead of time, see page 71.)

While the dough rises, make the apple filling: Heat the apples, sugar, and lemon juice together in a frying pan over medium-high heat until the sugar melts, stirring often. Continue cooking at a strong simmer, stirring occasionally, until the liquid is gone and the apples are soft, 5 to 7 minutes. Set aside to cool.

Transfer the dough to a lightly floured large cutting board and roll into a roughly 10 in/25 cm square, about ½ in/12 mm thick. Spread the cooled apples over half the dough, then sprinkle all of the cinnamon, then the flour, over the apples. Fold the empty half of the dough over the filling. Using a metal bench scraper or a large knife, cut the dough into shards ½ in/1 cm thick, first vertically and then horizontally, so you make a checkerboard pattern. Scoop and rearrange the dough, and cut again in both directions. Repeat. (This is not an exact process.) The mixture should be sticky and evenly spiced, and the dough should be chopped into tons of small pieces.

Using floured hands, form the dough into a log roughly 12 in/30 cm long by 3 in/8 cm in diameter, using a couple handfuls of extra flour to coat the log completely with flour. Slice it (at 1 in/2.5 cm intervals) into 12 equal pieces. Using floured hands, pat each piece of dough into a palm-size mound. Gently transfer the fritters to two lightly floured baking sheet, arranging them at least 2 in/5 cm apart, and let rise in the oven (with new boiling water), uncovered, for another 30 to 45 minutes, until doubled in size.

continued

▬ Using a candy thermometer to measure the temperature, heat oil (at least 2 in/5 cm deep) in a deep fryer, large pot, or high-sided frying pan over medium heat to 340°F/180°C. (For frying tips, see page 25.) When the fritters have doubled, carefully place a few in the oil, taking care not to overcrowd them, and fry for 60 to 75 seconds, or until light golden brown on the bottom. (Note that the fritters will look more brown when they're done than they do in the oil.) Carefully turn the fritters and fry for another 30 to 45 seconds, until golden on the second side, then transfer to a cooling rack set over a layer of paper towels/absorbent paper to cool, roundest side up. After the first batch, wait a moment or two, then check one fritter to verify that the dough has cooked through in the center. Repeat with the remaining fritters.

▬ While the fritters are still very warm, dip the entire rounded side of each into the warm glaze. (See page 29 for glazing tips.) Let dry on cooling racks, glazed side up, for 10 to 15 minutes, then serve.

BLACKBERRY FRITTERS

MAKES ONE DOZEN fritters

LIKE OUR APPLE FRITTERS, THESE BLACKBERRY FRITTERS ARE FUN TO MAKE
and impressive. The glaze, tinted with blackberry jam, is a favorite with the purple-loving set.

FRITTER DOUGH

1½ tbsp (two ¼ oz/7 g packages) active dry yeast

½ cup/120 ml very warm water (about 105°F/40°C)

¼ cup/50 g sugar, plus 2 tsp

¼ tsp baking powder

¼ tsp ground mace

1 tsp iodized salt

2¼ cups/310 g plus 4 to 6 tbsp bread/strong flour, plus more for rolling and cutting

2 tbsp shortening/vegetable lard, trans-fat-free preferred

1 large egg

¼ tsp vanilla extract

1½ cups/225 g frozen blackberries

1 tbsp sugar

2 tbsp bread/strong flour

Canola oil, for frying

Big batch Berry Glaze (page 134), made with blackberry jam

TIME
1 hour 5 minutes active time, plus glazing

EQUIPMENT
Metal bench scraper or large knife

To make the fritter dough: Whisk the yeast, water, and 2 tsp of the sugar together in the work bowl of a stand mixer and set aside for 5 minutes.

In a medium bowl, whisk together the remaining ¼ cup/50 g sugar, baking powder, mace, salt, and 2¼ cups/310 g of the bread/strong flour. Set aside.

Add the shortening/vegetable lard, egg, and vanilla to the foaming yeast mixture. Mix with the paddle attachment on low speed for 1 minute, to break up the shortening. Add about a third of the dry ingredients and mix until blended on low speed, then repeat with the second third of the dry ingredients.

Switch to the dough hook and add the remaining dry ingredients, mixing on low speed until no white spots remain each time, adding additional flour as necessary, until the dough is dry enough to clean the bottom of the bowl. Increase the speed to medium and knead for 2 more minutes. (It should be smooth like bread dough, but still a bit tacky.)

Transfer the dough to a baking sheet/tray sprinkled with 1 tbsp flour, shape into a flat 4 in/10 cm square, dust lightly with flour, cover with a dish/tea towel, and set aside.

Create a proofing box in your oven: Bring a large kettle of water to a boil. Pour 8 cups/2 L

continued

RAISED DOUGHNUTS

of the boiling water into a 9-by-13-in/25-by-35-cm (or similar) baking dish, and set it on the floor of your oven. Place the sheet/tray with the covered dough on the middle rack of the oven, close the door, and let the dough rise until doubled in size, about 1 hour. (For tips on making your dough ahead of time, see page 71.)

➥ Transfer the dough to a lightly floured large cutting board and roll into a roughly 10 in/25 cm square, about ½ in/12 mm thick. Spread the black-berries over half the dough, then sprinkle the sugar, then the flour, over the berries. Fold the empty half of the dough over the filling. Using a metal bench scraper or a large knife, cut the dough into shards ½ in/1 cm thick, first vertically, then horizon-tally, so you make a checkerboard pattern. Scoop and rearrange the dough, and cut again in both directions. Repeat until the berries are evenly distributed. (This is not an exact process.) The mixture should be sticky, and the dough should be chopped into tons of small pieces.

➥ Using floured hands, form the dough into a log roughly 12 in/30 cm long by 3 in/8 cm in diameter, using a couple handfuls of extra flour to coat the log completely with flour. (As the berries melt, the dough will get wet, so add flour as you go to prevent sticking.) Slice it (at 1 in/2.5 cm intervals) into 12 equal pieces. Using floured hands, pat each

piece of dough into a palm-size mound. Gently transfer the fritters to two lightly floured baking sheets/trays, arranging them at least 2 in/5 cm apart, and let rise in the oven (with new boiling water), uncovered, for another 30 to 45 minutes, until doubled in size.

➥ Using a candy thermometer to measure the temperature, heat oil (at least 2 in/5 cm deep) in a deep fryer, large pot, or high-sided frying pan over medium heat to 340°F/180°C. (For frying tips, see page 25.) When the fritters have doubled, carefully place a few in the oil, taking care not to overcrowd them, and fry for 60 to 75 seconds, or until light golden brown on the bottom. (Note that the fritters will look more brown when they're done than they do in the oil.) Carefully turn the fritters and fry for another 30 to 45 seconds, until golden on the second side, then transfer to a cooling rack set over a layer of paper towels/absorbent paper to cool, roundest side up. After the first batch, wait a moment or two, then check one fritter to verify that the dough has cooked through in the center. Repeat with the remaining fritters.

➥ While the fritters are still very warm, dip the entire rounded side of each into the warm Berry Glaze. (See page 29 for glazing tips.) Let dry on cooling racks, glazed side up, for 10 to 15 minutes.

OLD-FASHIONED
DOUGHNUTS

Old-fashioned doughnuts, fried at a lower temperature and turned twice to achieve their signature ridges and petals, were once called "crunchy" doughnuts because of their slightly crispier exteriors.

If you're planning to fry doughnuts for the next morning, old-fashioneds are a good choice. They hold up remarkably well because their cracks and crevices allow for plenty of glaze to sink in and around the cooked doughnut.

SOUR CREAM OLD-FASHIONED DOUGHNUTS

MAKES ONE DOZEN doughnuts and holes

TOP POT CO-OWNER MARK KLEBECK'S IDEAL DOUGHNUT EXPERIENCE REQUIRES a cup of hot black coffee and a plain old-fashioned. Made with sour cream and extra leavening and turned twice while frying, these doughnuts require a little more attention— but the ridges and petals that form during frying are perfect for catching extra glaze, which means glazed old-fashioneds keep better than yeast-raised or cake doughnuts.

Top your old-fashioneds with a small batch of Top Pot's Vanilla Doughnut Glaze (page 131), Simplest Vanilla Glaze (page 132), or Simple Chocolate Icing (page 126).

2¼ cups/255 g cake/soft-wheat flour, plus more for rolling and cutting	½ cup/100 g sugar	TIME
	2 tbsp shortening/vegetable lard, trans-fat-free preferred	1 hour active time, plus glazing or icing
1½ tsp baking powder		EQUIPMENT
1 tsp iodized salt	2 large egg yolks	Doughnut cutter
¾ tsp ground nutmeg	⅔ cup/165 ml sour cream	(or 2¾ in/7 cm and 1¼ in/3 cm round cutters)
	Canola oil, for frying	

➤ Sift the flour, baking powder, salt, and nutmeg together into a medium bowl, and set aside.

➤ In a stand mixer fitted with the paddle attachment, mix the sugar and shortening/vegetable lard for 1 minute on low speed, until sandy. Add the egg yolks, then mix for 1 more minute on medium speed, scraping the sides of the bowl with a rubber spatula if necessary, until the mixture is light colored and thick.

➤ Add the dry ingredients to the wet ingredients in three separate additions, alternating with the sour cream, mixing until just combined on low speed and scraping the sides of the bowl each time. The dough will be sticky, like cookie/biscuit dough.

➤ Transfer the dough to a clean bowl and refrigerate, covered with plastic wrap/cling film, for 45 minutes (or up to 24 hours).

➤ Using a candy thermometer to measure the temperature, heat oil (at least 2 in/5 cm deep) in a deep fryer, large pot, or high-sided frying pan to 325°F/165°C. (For frying tips, see page 25.) Roll out the chilled dough on a generously floured counter or cutting board to ½ in/12 mm thick, or about 8 in/20 cm in diameter, flouring the top of the dough and the rolling pin as necessary to prevent sticking. Cut into as many doughnuts and holes as possible, dipping the cutter into flour before each cut. Fold and gently reroll the dough, to make extra holes (working with floured hands makes the dough less sticky), and cut again.

➤ Shake any excess flour off the doughnuts before carefully adding them to the hot oil a few at a time, taking care not to crowd them. Once the doughnuts float, fry for 15 seconds, then gently flip them. Fry for 75 to 90 seconds, until golden brown and cracked, then flip and fry the first side again for 60 to 75 seconds, until golden. Transfer to a rack set over paper towels/absorbent paper.

PUMPKIN OLD-FASHIONED DOUGHNUTS

MAKES ONE DOZEN doughnuts and holes

EVERY FALL, SEATTLE AWAITS THE RELEASE OF OUR PUMPKIN
Old-Fashioneds—our classic glazed old-fashioned doughnut spiked with pumpkin
and spice. For a true taste of fall, serve them with warm apple cider.

PUMPKIN SPICE DOUGHNUTS

3 cups/355 g cake/soft-wheat flour,
plus more for rolling and cutting

2 tsp baking powder

1 tsp iodized salt

¾ tsp ground nutmeg

2 tsp pumpkin pie spice

½ cup/100 g sugar

2 tbsp shortening/vegetable lard,
trans-fat-free preferred

2 large egg yolks

⅔ cup/165 ml sour cream

½ cup/120 ml canned pumpkin

Canola oil, for frying

PUMPKIN GLAZE

4½ cups/1 lb/450 g confectioners'/
icing sugar, sifted

2 tsp light corn/golden syrup

¼ tsp iodized salt

1 tsp pumpkin pie spice

¼ cup/60 ml canned pumpkin

½ tsp vanilla extract

¼ cup/60 ml hot water

TIME
1 hour 5 minutes active
time, plus glazing

EQUIPMENT
Doughnut cutter
(or 2¾ in/7 cm and 1¼ in/3 cm
round cutters)

➡ To make the doughnut dough: Sift the flour, baking powder, salt, nutmeg, and pumpkin pie spice together into a medium bowl, and set aside.

➡ In a stand mixer fitted with the paddle attachment, mix the sugar and shortening/vegetable lard for 1 minute on low speed, until sandy. Add the egg yolks, then mix for 1 more minute on medium speed, scraping the sides of the bowl with a rubber spatula if necessary, until the mixture is light colored and thick.

➡ Add the dry ingredients to the wet ingredients in three separate additions, alternating with the sour cream and pumpkin, mixing until just combined on low speed and scraping the sides of the bowl each time. The dough will be sticky, like wet cookie/biscuit dough.

➡ Transfer the dough to a clean bowl and refrigerate, covered with plastic wrap/cling film, for 45 minutes (or up to 24 hours).

OLD-FASHIONED DOUGHNUTS

continued

➡ Meanwhile, make the pumpkin glaze: Place the confectioners'/icing sugar, corn/golden syrup, salt, pumpkin pie spice, pumpkin, and vanilla in the work bowl of a stand mixer fitted with the paddle attachment. With the machine on medium speed, add the water in a slow, steady stream, and blend until all of the sugar has been incorporated, scraping the bowl a few times if necessary. Set aside.

➡ Using a candy thermometer to measure the temperature, heat oil (at least 2 in/5 cm deep) in a deep fryer, large pot, or high-sided frying pan to 325°F/165°C. (For frying tips, see page 25.) Roll out the chilled dough on a generously floured counter or cutting board to $1/2$ in/12 mm thick, or about 8 in/20 cm in diameter, flouring the top of the dough and the rolling pin as necessary to prevent sticking. Cut into as many doughnuts and

holes as possible, dipping the cutter into flour before each cut. Fold and gently reroll the dough to make extra holes (working with floured hands makes the dough less sticky), and cut again.

➡ Shake any excess flour off the doughnuts before carefully adding them to the hot oil a few at a time, taking care not to crowd them. Once the doughnuts float, fry for 15 seconds, then gently flip them. Fry for 75 to 90 seconds, until golden brown and cracked, then flip and fry the first side again for 60 to 75 seconds, until golden. Transfer to a rack set over paper towels/absorbent paper.

➡ While the doughnuts are still quite hot, dip the side with the deepest cracks on each into the warm Pumpkin Glaze. (See page 29 for glazing tips.) Let dry on cooling racks, glazed side up, for about 15 minutes.

CHOCOLATE OLD-FASHIONED DOUGHNUTS

MAKES ONE DOZEN doughnuts and holes

TOP THESE WITH A SMALL BATCH OF TOP POT'S VANILLA DOUGHNUT GLAZE (PAGE 131), Simplest Vanilla Glaze (page 132), or Simple Chocolate Icing (page 126).

2 cups/225 g cake/soft-wheat flour, plus more for rolling and cutting

½ cup/50 g unsweetened Dutch-processed cocoa powder

1½ tsp baking powder

1 tsp iodized salt

¾ tsp ground nutmeg

½ cup/100 g sugar

2 tbsp shortening/vegetable lard, trans-fat-free preferred

2 large egg yolks

1 cup/240 ml sour cream

Canola oil, for frying

TIME
1 hour active time

EQUIPMENT
Doughnut cutter
(or 2¾ in/7 cm and 1¼ in/3 cm round cutters)

➥ Sift the flour, cocoa powder, baking powder, salt, and nutmeg together into a medium bowl, and set aside.

➥ In a stand mixer fitted with the paddle attachment, mix the sugar and shortening/vegetable lard for 1 minute on low speed, until sandy. Add the egg yolks, then mix for 1 more minute on medium speed, scraping the sides of the bowl with a rubber spatula if necessary, until the mixture is light colored and thick.

➥ Add the dry ingredients to the wet ingredients in three separate additions, alternating with the sour cream, mixing until just combined on low speed and scraping the sides of the bowl each time. The dough will be sticky, like cookie/biscuit dough.

➥ Transfer the dough to a clean bowl and refrigerate, covered with plastic wrap/cling film, for 45 minutes (or up to 24 hours).

➥ Using a candy thermometer to measure the temperature, heat oil (at least 2 in/5 cm deep) in a deep fryer, large pot, or high-sided frying pan to 325°F/165°C. (For frying tips, see page 25.) Roll out the chilled dough on a generously floured counter or cutting board to ½ in/12 mm thick, or about 8 in/20 cm in diameter, flouring the top of the dough and the rolling pin as necessary to prevent sticking. Cut into as many doughnuts and holes as possible, dipping the cutter into flour before each cut. Fold and gently reroll the dough to make extra holes (working with floured hands makes the dough less sticky), and cut again.

➥ Shake any excess flour off the doughnuts before carefully adding them to the hot oil a few at a time, taking care not to crowd them. Once the doughnuts float, fry for 15 seconds, then gently flip them. Fry for 75 to 90 seconds, until cracked, then flip and fry the first side again for 60 to 75 seconds. Transfer to a rack set over paper towels/absorbent paper.

FRENCH TOAST OLD-FASHIONED DOUGHNUTS

MAKES ONE DOZEN doughnuts and holes

FRENCH TOAST IS, ULTIMATELY, A VERY SIMPLE BREAKFAST:
bread is first soaked in a mixture of eggs, milk, cinnamon, sugar, and vanilla,
then toasted up in a pan and smothered with maple syrup.
Here's our doughnut-shaped version.

FRENCH TOAST DOUGHNUTS

2¼ cups/255 g cake/soft-wheat flour, plus more for rolling and cutting

1½ tsp baking powder

1 tsp iodized salt

¾ tsp ground nutmeg

2 tsp ground cinnamon

½ cup/100 g sugar

2 tbsp shortening/vegetable lard, trans-fat-free preferred

2 large egg yolks

1 tsp vanilla extract

1 tsp maple extract

⅔ cup/165 ml sour cream

Canola oil, for frying

MAPLE-CINNAMON GLAZE

3½ cups/350 g confectioners'/icing sugar, sifted

1½ tsp light corn/golden syrup

¼ tsp iodized salt

1 tsp ground cinnamon

1 tsp vanilla extract

½ tsp maple extract

⅓ cup/75 ml real maple syrup

¼ cup/60 ml warm milk

TIME
1 hour 5 minutes active time, plus glazing

EQUIPMENT
Doughnut cutter
(or 2¾ in/7 cm and 1¼ in/3 cm round cutters)

➡ To make the doughnut dough: Sift the flour, baking powder, salt, nutmeg, and cinnamon together into a medium bowl, and set aside.

➡ In a stand mixer fitted with the paddle attachment, mix the sugar and shortening/vegetable lard for 1 minute on low speed, until sandy. Add the egg yolks, then mix for 1 more minute on medium speed, scraping the sides of the bowl with a rubber spatula if necessary, until the mixture is light colored and thick. Stir in the vanilla and maple extract.

➡ Add the dry ingredients to the wet ingredients in three separate additions, alternating with the sour cream, mixing until just combined on low speed and scraping the sides of the bowl each time. The dough will be sticky, like cookie/biscuit dough.

➡ Transfer the dough to a clean bowl and refrigerate, covered with plastic wrap/cling film, for 45 minutes (or up to 24 hours).

➡ Meanwhile, make the glaze: Place the confectioners'/icing sugar, corn/golden syrup, salt, cinnamon, and vanilla and maple extract in the work bowl of a stand mixer fitted with the paddle attachment. With the machine on medium speed, add the maple syrup and milk in a slow, steady stream, and blend until all of the sugar has been incorporated, scraping the bowl a few times if necessary. Set aside.

➡ Using a candy thermometer to measure the temperature, heat oil (at least 2 in/5 cm deep) in a deep fryer, large pot, or high-sided frying pan to 325°F/165°C. Roll out the chilled dough on a generously floured counter or cutting board to ½ in/12 mm thick, or about 8 in/20 cm in diameter, flouring the top of the dough and the rolling pin as necessary to prevent sticking. Cut into as many doughnuts and holes as possible, dipping the cutter into flour before each cut. Fold and gently reroll the dough to make extra holes (working with floured hands makes the dough less sticky), and cut again.

➡ Shake any excess flour off the doughnuts before carefully adding them to the hot oil a few at a time, taking care not to crowd them. Once the doughnuts float, fry for 15 seconds, then gently flip them. Fry for 75 to 90 seconds, until golden brown and cracked, then flip and fry the first side again for 60 to 75 seconds, until golden. Transfer to a rack set over paper towels/absorbent paper.

➡ While the doughnuts are still quite hot, dip the side with the deepest cracks on each into the warm glaze. (See page 29 for glazing tips.) Let dry on cooling racks, glazed side up, for about 15 minutes.

OUTSIDE THE BOX

Here are a few recipes for doughnuts as you rarely
see them—baked into bread pudding, made
with whole-wheat/wholemeal or gluten-free flour,
or supersize, in the case of the Top Poppa, our giant
chocolate doughnut cake.

TOP POPPA
(GIANT CHOCOLATE DOUGHNUT CAKE)

MAKES 10 SERVINGS

MADE WITH THE DOUGHNUTS-AND-COFFEE LOVER'S BIRTHDAY IN MIND,
this moist sour cream cake has the hint of nutmeg Top Pot doughnuts are known for,
but doesn't require any frying. Bake it up, top it with coffee icing and sprinkles, and
it's bound to draw both attention and compliments. For an extra-fancy version, layer it
with the pastry cream used for the Bavarian Cream Bismarks (page 77).

CAKE

Vegetable oil spray

1¼ cups/145 g all-purpose/plain flour

½ cup/50 g unsweetened Dutch-processed cocoa powder

1½ tsp baking powder

½ tsp iodized salt

¾ tsp ground nutmeg

½ cup/115 g unsalted butter, at room temperature

½ cup/100 g sugar

2 large eggs

1 tsp vanilla extract

1¼ cups/300 ml sour cream

COFFEE ICING

2⅓ cups/235 g confectioners'/icing sugar, sifted

¾ tsp instant espresso powder

¼ tsp vanilla extract

Pinch salt

1 tsp light corn/golden syrup

3 tbsp leftover brewed coffee

Chocolate sprinkles/sugar strands (optional)

TIME

25 minutes active time

EQUIPMENT

10-cup/2 L tube pan/tin

➡ To make cake: Preheat the oven to 350°F/180°C/gas 4. Spray a 10-cup/2 L tube pan/tin with the vegetable oil spray, and set aside.

➡ Sift the flour, cocoa powder, baking powder, salt, and nutmeg into a medium bowl. Set aside.

➡ In the work bowl of a stand mixer fitted with the paddle attachment (or using a handheld mixer), cream the butter and sugar on medium speed until light, about 2 minutes. Add the eggs, one at a time, mixing after each addition, then add the vanilla, and mix to blend. With the machine on low speed, add half the dry ingredients, then the sour cream, then the remaining dry ingredients, mixing just until the flour is incorporated.

➡ Transfer the batter to the prepared pan/tin, smoothing it flat with a spoon. Bake for 25 to 30 minutes, until the top is puffed and a bit cracked and a wooden skewer inserted into the thickest part comes out clean.

➡ Cool the cake in the pan/tin for 10 minutes. Run a small knife or spatula around the edges, then invert the cake first onto a cooling rack, then again onto a serving plate. Set aside.

➡ While the cake cools, make the icing: Sift the confectioners'/icing sugar into the work bowl of a stand mixer fitted with the paddle attachment.

Add the espresso powder, vanilla, salt, corn/golden syrup, and coffee, then mix on low speed until all of the sugar is incorporated. (You can also do this in a bowl, stirring with a whisk by hand.)

➡ Spread the icing over the top of the cooled cake, allowing some of it to drip down the sides. Top immediately with sprinkles/sugar strands, if using. Allow the icing to set for at least 20 minutes before serving.

DOUGHNUT BREAD PUDDING

MAKES 6 SERVINGS

IF YOU'RE A BREAD PUDDING FAN, NOTHING TOPS A SLICE MADE WITH DAY-OLD
yeast-raised doughnuts—except, perhaps, a drizzle of a warm vanilla icing (or a scoop of vanilla
ice cream). And because some of bread pudding's typical ingredients are already right in the doughnuts, this dessert is quick to make. Stir in 1/2 cup/85 g raisins or chocolate chips, if you'd like.

DOUGHNUT BREAD PUDDING

Butter for the pan/tin

6 cups/300 g 1 in/2.5 cm cubes
leftover raised doughnuts (about
4 whole), such as Raised Glazed
Ring (page 72), Raspberry Bullseyes
(page 81), Apple Fritters (page 88),
or Maple Bars (page 83)

4 large eggs

2 tbsp dark rum, or 1/2 tsp rum
extract

1/2 tsp ground cinnamon

1/4 cup/50 g sugar

1 tsp vanilla extract

1 cup/240 ml whole milk

3/4 cup/180 ml heavy (whipping)/
double cream

ICING

1 cup/100 g confectioners'/
icing sugar, sifted

1 tsp vanilla extract

1 1/2 tbsp hot water

TIME
15 minutes active time

EQUIPMENT
9-by-5-in/23-by-12-cm
loaf pan/tin

➡ To make the bread pudding: Preheat the oven to
350°F/180°C/gas 4. Grease a 9-by-5-in/23-by-12-cm
loaf pan/tin with the butter, and fill with the cubed
leftover doughnuts. Set aside.

➡ In a mixing bowl, whisk the eggs, rum, cinnamon, sugar, and vanilla until well blended. Add the
milk and cream, whisk to blend, and pour over
the doughnuts, turning the top pieces so that all
of the doughnuts are soaked in the wet mixture.

➡ Bake for 45 to 50 minutes, or until browned on
top and firm in the center. Let cool for 10 minutes
in the pan.

➡ While the pudding cools, make the icing: Whisk
the icing ingredients together in a small bowl until
smooth.

➡ Serve the pudding in thick slices, still warm,
drizzled with the icing.

WHOLE-WHEAT
RAISED GLAZED RINGS

MAKES ONE DOZEN plus more if rerolled (plus holes)

TOP POT DOESN'T SERVE WHOLE-WHEAT DOUGHNUTS IN ITS CAFES, BUT AT HOME
we often bake with whole-wheat flour. This slightly healthier version of our classic
glazed raised rings is made with white whole-wheat flour—we challenge your
eaters to notice a difference. You can use this dough for any of our raised doughnut
recipes, such as Maple Bars (page 83) or Pershings (page 85). See "Leaving
Your Mark" on page 79 to learn how to transfer the raised rings into the hot oil.

3 tbsp (four ¼ oz/7g packets) active dry yeast

1 cup/240 ml very warm water (about 105°F/40°C)

½ cup/100 g sugar, plus 1 tbsp

½ tsp baking powder

½ tsp ground mace

2 tsp iodized salt

2 cups/275 g white whole-wheat/ wholemeal flour

2 to 2½ cups/275 to 340 g bread/ strong flour, plus more for rolling and cutting

¼ cup/55 g shortening/vegetable lard, trans-fat-free preferred

3 large egg yolks

½ tsp vanilla extract

Canola oil, for frying

Small batch Simplest Vanilla Glaze (page 132) or Top Pot's Vanilla Doughnut Glaze (page 131)

TIME
1 hour active time,
plus glazing

EQUIPMENT
Doughnut cutter
(or 2¾ in/7 cm and 1¼ in/3 cm
round cutters)

➡ Whisk the yeast, water, and 1 tbsp of the sugar together in the work bowl of a stand mixer and set aside for 5 minutes.

➡ In a large bowl, whisk together the remaining ½ cup/100 g sugar, baking powder, mace, salt, white whole-wheat/wholemeal flour, and 2 cups/ 275 g of the bread/strong flour. Set aside.

➡ Add the shortening/vegetable lard, egg yolks, and vanilla to the foaming yeast mixture. Mix with the paddle attachment on low speed for 1 minute,

to break up the shortening. Add about a third of the dry ingredients and mix until blended on low speed, then repeat with the second third of the dry ingredients.

➡ Switch to the dough hook and add the remaining dry ingredients, mixing on low speed until no white spots remain each time, adding additional flour as necessary, until the dough is dry enough to clean the bottom of the bowl. Increase the speed to medium and knead for 2 more minutes. (It should be smooth like bread dough, but still a bit tacky.)

➡ Transfer the dough to a baking sheet/tray sprinkled with 1 tbsp bread/strong flour, shape into a flat disk 6 in/15 cm in diameter, dust lightly with flour, cover with a dish/tea towel, and set aside.

➡ Create a proofing box in your oven: Bring a large kettle of water to a boil. Pour 8 cups/2 L of the boiling water into a 9-by-13-in/25-by-35-cm (or similar) baking dish, and set it on the floor of your oven. Place the sheet/tray with the covered dough on the middle rack of the oven, close the door, and let the dough rise until doubled in size, about 1 hour. (For tips on making your dough ahead of time, see page 71.)

➡ Transfer the dough to a lightly floured work surface and roll into a roughly 12 in/30 cm circle, about 1/2 in/12 mm thick, with a lightly floured rolling pin. Cut into 12 doughnuts, flouring the cutter before each cut. (Reroll the dough for addi tional doughnuts.) Gently transfer the doughnuts (and holes) to two baking sheets/trays sprinkled with 2 tbsp bread/strong flour each, arranging

them at least 2 in/5 cm apart, and let rise in the oven (with new boiling water), uncovered, for another 30 to 45 minutes, until doubled in size.

➡ Using a candy thermometer to measure the temperature, heat oil (at least 2 in/5 cm deep) in a deep fryer, large pot, or high-sided frying pan over medium heat to 350°F/180°C. (For frying tips, see page 25.) When the doughnuts have doubled, carefully place a few in the oil, taking care not to overcrowd them, and fry for about 30 seconds, or until light golden brown on the bottom. (Note that the doughnuts will look more brown when they're done than they do in the oil.) Carefully turn the doughnuts and fry for another 20 to 30 seconds, until golden on the second side, then transfer to a cooling rack set over a layer of paper towels/ absorbent paper to cool, rounded side up.

➡ While the doughnuts are still very warm, dip the rounded side of each into the warm glaze. (See page 29 for glazing tips.) Let dry on cooling racks, glazed side up, for 10 to 15 minutes, then serve.

BAKED RAISED DOUGHNUTS

MAKES ONE DOZEN plus more if rerolled (plus holes)

COATED WITH CINNAMON SUGAR, THESE DOUGHNUTS ARE BAKED, NOT FRIED—
which means less mess, and more kid-friendliness. It's not necessary, but here's your
chance to use a doughnut pan. Equipped with six indentations for doughnuts, these nonstick
pans yield baked doughnuts that are rounded on both the top and the bottom.
Of course, you could ice or glaze these doughnuts, instead of using the cinnamon sugar.

BAKED DOUGHNUTS

2 tbsp plus 1 tsp (three ¼ oz/7 g packages) active dry yeast

1 cup/240 ml very warm water (about 105°F/40°C)

½ cup/100 g sugar, plus 1 tbsp

½ tsp baking powder

½ tsp ground mace

2 tsp iodized salt

4 to 4½ cups/550 to 620 g bread/ strong flour, plus more for rolling and cutting

¼ cup/55 g shortening/vegetable lard, trans-fat-free preferred

3 large egg yolks

½ tsp vanilla extract

TOPPING

2 cups/400 g sugar

1 tbsp ground cinnamon

Vegetable oil spray

¼ cup/55 g unsalted butter, melted

TIME
1 hour active time.

EQUIPMENT
Doughnut cutter
(or 2¾ in/7 cm and 1¼ in/3 cm
round cutters)

➡ To make the doughnut dough: Whisk the yeast, water, and 1 tbsp of the sugar together in the work bowl of a stand mixer and set aside for 5 minutes.

➡ In a large bowl, whisk together the remaining ½ cup/100 g sugar, baking powder, mace, salt, and 4 cups/550 g of the bread/strong flour. Set aside.

➡ Add the shortening/vegetable lard, egg yolks, and vanilla to the foaming yeast mixture. Mix with the paddle attachment on low speed for 1 minute, to break up the shortening. Add about a third of

the dry ingredients and mix until blended on low speed, then repeat with the second third of the dry ingredients.

➡ Switch to the dough hook and add the remaining dry ingredients, mixing on low speed until no white spots remain each time, adding additional flour, as necessary, until the dough is dry enough to clean the bottom of the bowl. Increase the speed to medium and knead for 2 more minutes. (It should be smooth like bread dough, but still a bit tacky.)

➡ Transfer the dough to a baking sheet/tray sprinkled with 1 tbsp flour, shape into a flat disk 6 in/15 cm in diameter, dust lightly with flour, cover with a dish/tea towel, and set aside.

➡ Create a proofing box in your oven: Bring a large kettle of water to a boil. Pour 8 cups/2 L of the boiling water into a 9-by-13-in/25-by-35-cm (or similar) baking dish, and set it on the floor of your oven. Place the sheet/tray with the covered dough on the middle rack of the oven, close the door, and let the dough rise until doubled in size, about 1 hour.

➡ Transfer the dough to a lightly floured work surface and roll into a roughly 12 in/30 cm circle, about ½ in/12 mm thick, with a lightly floured rolling pin. Cut into 12 doughnuts, flouring the cutter before each cut. (Reroll the dough for additional doughnuts.) Gently transfer the doughnuts (and holes) to two or three clean baking sheets/trays, arranging them at least 2 in/5 cm apart, and let rise in the oven (with new boiling water), uncovered, for another 30 to 45 minutes, until doubled in size.

➡ Meanwhile, make the topping: Mix the sugar and cinnamon together in a large bowl. Set aside.

➡ Preheat the oven to 350°F/180°C/gas 4. When hot, spray the tops of the doughnuts with vegetable oil spray. Bake for 12 to 15 minutes, or until the tops are lightly toasted, rotating the pans halfway through.

➡ While the doughnuts are still warm, brush with the melted butter on all sides, then toss them in the cinnamon sugar. Serve immediately.

GLUTEN-FREE CHOCOLATE
CAKE DOUGHNUTS

MAKES ONE DOZEN when rerolled, plus a few holes

ALTHOUGH WE DON'T SERVE GLUTEN-FREE PRODUCTS IN OUR CAFES,
we feel that everyone deserves a good doughnut—even those with dietary restrictions.
This version, made with an all-purpose gluten-free baking mix sold in the baking aisle
of many large supermarkets, yields deeply chocolaty doughnuts that roll out easily.

See page 122 for glazing or icing recipes, and page 140 for resources for
gluten-free flours and xanthan gum, a fine powder that gives baked goods a texture
more similar to those made with gluten.

1¾ cups/220 g gluten-free all-purpose baking flour (such as Bob's Red Mill), plus more for rolling and cutting	¾ tsp ground nutmeg	TIME
	½ cup/100 g sugar	1 hour active time, plus glazing or icing
	2 tbsp shortening/vegetable lard, trans-fat-free preferred	
½ cup/50 g unsweetened Dutch-processed cocoa powder	3 large egg yolks	EQUIPMENT
1 tsp xanthan gum	1 tsp vanilla extract	Doughnut cutter (or 2¾ in/7 cm and 1¼ in/3 cm round cutters)
1 tsp baking powder	⅔ cup/165 ml whole milk	
1 tsp iodized salt	Canola oil, for frying	

➡ Sift the gluten-free flour, cocoa powder, xanthan gum, baking powder, salt, and nutmeg together into a medium bowl, and set aside.

➡ In a stand mixer fitted with the paddle attachment, mix the sugar and shortening/vegetable lard for 1 minute on low speed, until sandy. Add the egg yolks one at a time, then mix for 1 more minute on medium speed, scraping the sides of the bowl with a rubber spatula if necessary, until the mixture is light colored and thick. Mix in the vanilla.

➡ Add the dry ingredients to the wet ingredients in three separate additions, alternating with the milk, mixing until just combined on low speed each time. The dough will be sticky, like a wet cookie/biscuit dough.

➡ Transfer the dough to a clean bowl and refrigerate, covered with plastic wrap/cling film, for 1 hour (or up to 24 hours).

➡ Using a candy thermometer to measure the temperature, heat oil (at least 2 in/5 cm deep) in a deep fryer, large pot, or high-sided frying pan over

continued

OUTSIDE THE BOX

medium heat to 370°F/185°C. (For frying tips, see page 25.) Roll out the chilled dough on a counter or cutting board sprinkled with 2 to 3 tbsp gluten-free flour to ³/₈ in/1 cm thick, or about 9 in/22 cm in diameter, flouring the top of the dough and the rolling pin as necessary to prevent sticking. Cut into as many doughnuts and holes as possible, dipping the cutter into flour before each cut. Fold and gently reroll the dough to make extra holes (working with floured hands makes the dough less sticky), and cut again.

➡ Shake any excess flour off the doughnuts before carefully adding them to the hot oil a few at a time, taking care not to crowd them. Once the doughnuts float, fry for about 60 seconds per side—you won't be able to see when the doughnuts brown because of the chocolate, but you'll see a change in texture. Drain on paper towels/absorbent paper.

GLUTEN-FREE OLD-FASHIONED CAKE DOUGHNUTS

MAKES ONE DOZEN if rerolled, plus a few holes

ALTHOUGH THEY WON'T SPLIT QUITE LIKE OLD-FASHIONEDS MADE WITH WHEAT FLOUR, these wheat-free doughnuts, moistened with sour cream, have the same tangy flavor and moist texture. Top your old-fashioneds with a small batch of Top Pot's Vanilla Doughnut Glaze (page 131), Simplest Vanilla Glaze (page 132), or Simple Chocolate Icing (page 126).

2 cups/255 g gluten-free all-purpose baking flour (such as Bob's Red Mill), plus more for rolling and cutting

1½ tsp baking powder

1 tsp xanthan gum

1 tsp iodized salt

¾ tsp ground nutmeg

½ cup/100 g sugar

2 tbsp shortening/vegetable lard, trans-fat-free preferred

2 large egg yolks

1 cup/240 ml sour cream

Canola oil, for frying

TIME
1 hour active time, plus glazing or icing

EQUIPMENT
Doughnut cutter
(or 2¾ in/7 cm and 1¼ in/3 cm round cutters)

➡ Sift the gluten-free flour, baking powder, xanthan gum, salt, and nutmeg together into a medium bowl, and set aside.

➡ In a stand mixer fitted with the paddle attachment, mix the sugar and shortening/vegetable lard for 1 minute on low speed, until sandy. Add the egg yolks, then mix for 1 more minute on medium speed, scraping the sides of the bowl with a rubber spatula if necessary, until the mixture is light colored and thick.

➡ Add the dry ingredients to the wet ingredients in three separate additions, alternating with the sour cream, mixing until just combined on low speed each time. The dough will be sticky, like cookie/biscuit dough.

➡ Transfer the dough to a clean bowl and refrigerate, covered with plastic wrap/cling film, for 45 minutes (or up to 24 hours).

➡ Using a candy thermometer to measure the temperature, heat oil (at least 2 in/5 cm deep) in a deep fryer, large pot, or high-sided frying pan to 350°F/180°C. Roll out the chilled dough on a counter or cutting board generously floured with gluten-free flour to ½ in/12 mm thick, or about 8 in/20 cm in diameter, flouring the top of the dough and the rolling pin as necessary to prevent sticking. Cut into as many doughnuts and holes as possible, dipping the cutter into flour before each cut. Fold and gently reroll the dough to make extra holes (working with floured hands makes the dough less sticky), and cut again.

continued

■ Shake any excess flour off the doughnuts before carefully adding them to the hot oil a few at a time, taking care not to crowd them. Once the doughnuts float, fry for 60 to 75 seconds per side, or until deep golden brown on both sides. Drain on paper towels/absorbent paper.

POWDERED SUGAR MINIS

MAKES ABOUT 18 mini doughnuts

SOMETIMES A WHOLE DOUGHNUT IS TOO MUCH—AND, WE ADMIT,
we're all intoxicated by anything that comes in miniature. These are our basic spice
cake doughnuts, made smaller (from a small batch), and tossed in confectioners'/icing
sugar. To make a large batch of them, follow the master recipe for Basic Spice
Cake Doughnuts (page 34), and use the rolling and frying directions that follow.

Mini doughnut cutters are tough to find—to improvise, use a clean
tomato paste can for the outside ring and the end of a turkey baster, a wide straw,
or the small end of a large pastry/piping bag tip for the inside ring.

1½ cups/190 g cake/soft-wheat flour, plus more for rolling and cutting	1 tbsp shortening/vegetable lard, trans-fat-free preferred	TIME
		1 hour 5 minutes active time
½ tsp baking powder	2 large egg yolks	
½ tsp iodized salt	⅓ cup/75 ml whole milk	EQUIPMENT
¼ tsp ground nutmeg	Canola oil, for frying	Mini doughnut cutter (or 2 in/5 cm and ½ in/1 cm round cutters)
⅔ cup/130 g sugar	1 cup/100 g confectioners'/icing sugar, sifted	

➤ Sift the flour, baking powder, salt, and nutmeg together into a medium bowl, and set aside.

➤ In a stand mixer fitted with the paddle attachment, mix the sugar and shortening/vegetable lard for 1 minute on low speed, until sandy. Add the egg yolks, then mix for 1 more minute on medium speed, scraping the sides of the bowl with a rubber spatula if necessary, until the mixture is light colored and thick.

➤ Add half of the dry ingredients, then the milk, then the remaining dry ingredients, mixing until just combined on low speed each time. The dough will be very sticky, like very wet cookie/biscuit dough.

➤ Transfer the dough to a clean bowl and refrigerate, covered directly with plastic wrap/cling film, for 45 minutes (or up to 24 hours).

➤ Using a candy thermometer to measure the temperature, heat oil (at least 2 in/5 cm deep) in a deep fryer, large pot, or high-sided frying pan over medium heat to 350°F/180°C. (For frying tips, see page 25.) Roll out the chilled dough on a counter or cutting board floured with about 3 tbsp cake/soft-wheat flour to ⅜ in/1 cm thick, or about 7 in/17 cm in diameter, flouring the top of the dough and the rolling pin with another tablespoon of

continued

OUTSIDE THE BOX

flour, or as necessary to prevent sticking—this is a soft, wet dough. Cut into doughnuts, using the big cutter for the outside ring and the small cutter for the inside ring if you don't have a doughnut cutter, making as many doughnuts and holes as possible, dipping the cutter into flour before each cut. Fold, quickly knead, and gently reroll the leftover dough to make extra holes (working with floured hands makes the dough less sticky), and cut again.

■ Shake any excess flour off the doughnuts before carefully adding them to the hot oil, five or six at a time, taking care not to crowd them. Once the doughnuts float, fry for 45 to 60 seconds per side, or until deep golden brown on both sides. Drain on paper towels/absorbent paper.

■ When the doughnuts are completely cool, transfer the confectioners'/icing sugar to a large brown paper bag. Add the doughnuts, seal the top, and shake to coat the doughnuts with the sugar. Serve immediately.

Icings, Glazes, and Toppings

Let's face it: most of us pick out our doughnuts because of what's on top.

Whether you're a sprinkle junkie or prefer a good, simple glaze, you'll want to plan out your dough-nuts' wardrobe in advance. If you plan to glaze, you'll need to make the glaze just before frying (or if you have help, while frying) the doughnuts, so you can dip piping-hot doughnuts into the warm glaze as soon as you can touch them. For icing doughnuts, the doughnuts themselves should be cool, but the icing is much easier to work with if it's still warm. (See page 30 for directions on how to thin, thicken, and rewarm glazes and icings.) Also plan ahead for any sprinkles or toppings, as

they need to be applied as soon as possible after you dip the doughnuts into the icing. See page 138 for great creative topping ideas.

Keep in mind that the icing and glaze recipes used previously in this book may be combined with almost any doughnut—try dipping Classic Twists (page 75) in Coconut Glaze (page 38), slathering Maple Bars (page 83) with Dulce de Leche Icing (page 68) instead of the traditional maple, or coat-ing Whole-Wheat Raised Glazed Rings (page 110) in Pumpkin Glaze (page 99).

TOP POT'S WHITE DOUGHNUT ICING

MAKES ENOUGH FOR ONE DOZEN doughnuts

3¼ cups/320 g confectioners'/icing sugar, sifted

1½ tsp light corn/golden syrup

¼ tsp iodized salt

¼ tsp vanilla extract

1 tbsp granulated sugar

½ tsp powdered agar

⅓ cup/75 ml plus 1 tbsp water

TIME
15 minutes active time, plus icing

➡ Place the confectioners'/icing sugar, corn/golden syrup, salt, and vanilla in a large mixing bowl or in the work bowl of a stand mixer fitted with the paddle attachment. Set aside.

➡ Next, make a syrup with the granulated sugar, agar, and water. Whisk the granulated sugar, agar, and water together in a small saucepan. Bring to a boil over high heat, then reduce the heat to medium and simmer for 1 minute, stirring occasionally. Add the syrup to the confectioners'/icing sugar bowl. Using a whisk, or with the machine on low speed, blend until the mixture is smooth and all of the sugar has been incorporated, scraping the sides of the bowl with a rubber spatula if necessary.

➡ To ice, immediately dip one side of each cooled doughnut into the warm icing, and let dry for 10 to 15 minutes before serving.

➡ For icing tips, see page 29.

TOP POT'S CHOCOLATE DOUGHNUT ICING

MAKES ENOUGH FOR ONE DOZEN doughnuts

3¼ cups/320 g confectioners'/
icing sugar, sifted

1½ tsp light corn/golden syrup

¼ tsp iodized salt

¼ tsp vanilla extract

1 tbsp granulated sugar

½ tsp powdered agar

⅓ cup/75 ml plus 1 tbsp water

⅔ cup/115 g semisweet/plain chocolate chips or chopped semisweet/
plain chocolate, melted

TIME
15 minutes active time,
plus icing

➡ Place the confectioners'/icing sugar, corn/golden syrup, salt, and vanilla in a large mixing bowl or in the work bowl of a stand mixer fitted with the paddle attachment. Set aside.

➡ Next, make a syrup with the granulated sugar, agar, and water: Whisk the granulated sugar, agar, and water together in a small saucepan. Bring to a boil over high heat, then reduce the heat to medium and simmer for 1 minute, stirring occasionally. Add the syrup to the confectioners'/icing sugar bowl. Using a whisk, or with the machine on low speed, blend until the mixture is smooth and all of the sugar has been incorporated, scraping the sides of the bowl with a rubber spatula if necessary. Add the chocolate, and stir to combine completely.

➡ To ice, immediately dip one side of each cooled doughnut into the warm icing, and let dry for 10 to 15 minutes before serving.

➡ For icing tips, see page 29

SIMPLE WHITE ICING

MAKES ENOUGH FOR ONE DOZEN doughnuts

4½ cups/1 lb/450 g confectioners'/
icing sugar, sifted

1½ tsp light corn/golden syrup

¼ tsp iodized salt

¼ tsp vanilla extract

⅓ cup/75 ml plus 1 tbsp hot water,
plus more if needed

TIME
5 minutes
active time,
plus icing

⮞ Place the confectioners'/icing sugar, corn/
golden syrup, salt, vanilla, and hot water in a
large mixing bowl or in the work bowl of a stand
mixer fitted with the paddle attachment. Using
a whisk, or with the machine on low speed, blend
until the mixture is smooth and all of the sugar
has been incorporated, scraping the sides of the
bowl with a rubber spatula if necessary. If the
icing seems too thick, add more hot water, a
teaspoon at a time.

⮞ To ice, dip one side of each cooled doughnut into the warm icing, and let dry for 10 to
15 minutes before serving.

⮞ For icing tips, see page 29.

SIMPLE CHOCOLATE ICING

MAKES ENOUGH FOR ONE DOZEN doughnuts

4½ cups/1 lb/450 g confectioners'/
icing sugar, sifted

1½ tsp light corn/golden syrup

¼ tsp iodized salt

¼ tsp vanilla extract

⅓ cup/75 ml plus 2 tbsp hot water,
plus more if needed

⅔ cup/115 g semisweet/plain
chocolate chips or chopped
semisweet/plain chocolate, melted

TIME
10 minutes
active time,
plus icing

⮞ Place the confectioners'/icing sugar, corn/
golden syrup, salt, vanilla, and hot water in a
large mixing bowl or in the work bowl of a stand
mixer fitted with the paddle attachment. Using
a whisk, or with the machine on low speed, blend
until the mixture is smooth and all of the sugar
has been incorporated, scraping the sides of
the bowl with a rubber spatula if necessary. Add
the chocolate, and stir to combine completely.
If the icing seems too thick, add more hot water,
a teaspoon at a time.

⮞ To ice, dip one side of each cooled doughnut into the warm icing, and let dry for 10 to
15 minutes before serving.

⮞ For icing tips, see page 29.

CARAMEL ICING

MAKES ENOUGH FOR ONE DOZEN doughnuts

THE THICKNESS OF THIS ICING DEPENDS ON HOW WARM THE CARAMEL is when you add it. If you wait a bit too long and it seems thick, add hot water, a teaspoon at a time, until it reaches the desired consistency.

Take care when adding the cream to the caramel; it tends to spatter and bubble a bit.

For a salted caramel icing, double the salt in the icing and sprinkle chunky sea salt onto the doughnuts before the icing dries.

ICING BASE	CARAMEL	TIME
4½ cups/1 lb/450 g confectioners'/icing sugar, sifted	½ cup/100 g sugar	30 minutes active time, plus icing
1½ tsp light corn/golden syrup	¼ cup/60 ml water	
¼ tsp iodized salt	¼ cup/60 ml heavy (whipping)/double cream	
¼ tsp vanilla extract		
⅓ cup/75 ml plus 1 tbsp hot water, plus more if needed		

First, make the icing base: Place the confectioners'/icing sugar, corn/golden syrup, salt, vanilla, and hot water in a large mixing bowl or in the work bowl of a stand mixer fitted with the paddle attachment. Using a whisk, or with the machine on low speed, blend until the mixture is smooth and all of the sugar has been incorporated, scraping the sides of the bowl with a rubber spatula if necessary.

Next, make the caramel: Combine the sugar and water in a small, nonreactive saucepan over high heat. Stir until the sugar dissolves, then cook at a high simmer, undisturbed, swirling the pan (but not stirring) occasionally until the caramel turns an amber color, 6 to 8 minutes. Remove from the heat. While whisking (or swirling the pan by its handle), carefully add the cream in a slow, steady stream, and continue whisking until the caramel stops bubbling. Let cool for 10 minutes.

Add the warm caramel to the icing base, and stir to blend. If the icing seems too thick, add more hot water, a teaspoon at a time.

To ice, dip one side of each cooled doughnut into the warm icing, and let dry for 10 to 15 minutes before serving.

For icing tips, see page 29.

PINK ICING

MAKES ENOUGH FOR ONE DOZEN doughnuts

MAKES ENOUGH FOR ONE DOZEN doughnuts

4½ cups/1 lb/450 g confectioners'/icing sugar, sifted	TIME
1½ tsp light corn/golden syrup	5 minutes active time, plus icing
¼ tsp iodized salt	
¼ tsp vanilla extract	
1 to 3 drops red food coloring	
⅓ cup/75 ml plus 1 tbsp hot water, plus more if needed	

➡ Place the confectioners'/icing sugar, corn/golden syrup, salt, vanilla, red food coloring, and hot water in a large mixing bowl or in the work bowl of a stand mixer fitted with the paddle attachment. (We'd use 1 drop of food coloring for light pink, 2 for a medium pink, and 3 for dark pink.) Using a whisk, or with the machine on low speed, blend until the mixture is smooth and all of the sugar has been incorporated, scraping the sides of the bowl with a rubber spatula if necessary. If the icing seems too thick, add more hot water, a teaspoon at a time.

➡ To ice, dip one side of each cooled doughnut into the warm icing, and let dry for 10 to 15 minutes before serving.

➡ For icing tips, see page 29.

MAPLE ICING

MAKES ENOUGH FOR ONE DOZEN doughnuts

4½ cups/1 lb/450 g confectioners'/icing sugar, sifted	TIME
1½ tsp light corn/golden syrup	5 minutes active time, plus icing
¼ tsp iodized salt	
¼ tsp vanilla extract	
¾ tsp maple extract	
⅓ cup/75 ml plus 1 tbsp hot water, plus more if needed	

➡ Place the confectioners'/icing sugar, corn/golden syrup, salt, vanilla and maple extracts, and hot water in a large mixing bowl or in the work bowl of a stand mixer fitted with the paddle attachment. Using a whisk, or with the machine on low speed, blend until the mixture is smooth and all of the sugar has been incorporated, scraping the sides of the bowl with a rubber spatula if necessary. If the icing seems too thick, add more hot water, a teaspoon at a time.

➡ To ice, dip one side of each cooled doughnut into the warm icing, and let dry for 10 to 15 minutes before serving.

➡ For icing tips, see page 29.

PEANUT BUTTER ICING

MAKES ENOUGH FOR ONE DOZEN doughnuts

½ cup/120 ml boiling water, plus
more if needed

¼ cup/60 ml smooth peanut butter,
or other smooth nut butter

4½ cups/1 lb/450 g confectioners'/
icing sugar, sifted, plus more
if needed

1½ tsp light corn/golden syrup

¼ tsp iodized salt

¼ tsp vanilla extract

TIME
10 minutes active time,
plus icing

➥ In a small bowl, stir the water and the peanut butter with a fork until completely smooth.

➥ Place 4½ cups/450 g confectioners'/icing sugar and the corn/golden syrup, salt, and vanilla in a large mixing bowl or in the work bowl of a stand mixer fitted with the paddle attachment. Add the peanut butter mixture. Using a whisk, or with the machine on low speed, blend until the mixture is smooth and all of the sugar has been incorporated, scraping the sides of the bowl with a rubber spatula if necessary. Depending on your brand of peanut or nut butter, you may need to add a bit more water or confectioners'/icing sugar.

➥ To ice, dip one side of each cooled doughnut into the warm icing, and let dry for 10 to 15 minutes before serving.

➥ For icing tips, see page 29.

TRIPLE ORANGE ICING

MAKES ENOUGH FOR ONE DOZEN doughnuts

4½ cups/1 lb/450 g confectioners'/
icing sugar, sifted

1½ tsp light corn/golden syrup

¼ tsp iodized salt

¼ tsp vanilla extract

¼ tsp orange extract

Grated zest of 1 large orange

⅓ cup/75 ml plus 1 tbsp freshly
squeezed orange juice, plus more
if needed

TIME
10 minutes active time,
plus icing

➡ Place the confectioners'/icing sugar, corn/golden syrup, salt, vanilla, orange extract, orange zest, and orange juice in a large mixing bowl or in the work bowl of a stand mixer fitted with the paddle attachment. Using a whisk, or with the machine on low speed, blend until the mixture is smooth and all of the sugar has been incorporated, scraping the sides of the bowl with a rubber spatula if necessary. If the icing seems too thick, add more orange juice, a teaspoon at a time.

➡ To ice, dip one side of each cooled doughnut into the warm icing, and let dry for 10 to 15 minutes before serving.

➡ For icing tips, see page 29.

Note: This icing depends on orange juice, zest, and extract for a big punch of flavor. It also has a slight orange color, but you can always make it more orange by adding a drop or two each of yellow and red food coloring.

TOP POT'S VANILLA DOUGHNUT GLAZE

SMALL BATCH MAKES ENOUGH FOR ONE DOZEN cake or ring-shaped doughnuts
BIG BATCH MAKES ENOUGH FOR ONE DOZEN large doughnuts (bars, pershings, twists, fritters, or bullseyes)

SMALL BATCH	BIG BATCH	TIME
2 cups/200 g confectioners'/icing sugar, sifted	4½ cups/1 lb/450 g confectioners'/icing sugar, sifted	15 minutes active time, plus icing
1½ tsp light corn/golden syrup	1 tbsp light corn/golden syrup	
¼ tsp iodized salt	½ tsp iodized salt	
½ tsp vanilla extract	1 tsp vanilla extract	
1 tbsp granulated sugar	2 tbsp plus 1 tsp granulated sugar	
⅓ tsp powdered agar	1¼ tsp powdered agar	
⅓ cup/75 ml plus 1 tbsp water	⅔ cup/165 ml water	

➡ Place the confectioners'/icing sugar, corn/golden syrup, salt, and vanilla in a large mixing bowl or in the work bowl of a stand mixer fitted with the paddle attachment. Set aside.

➡ Next, make a syrup with the granulated sugar, agar, and water: Whisk the granulated sugar, agar, and water together in a small saucepan. Bring to a boil over high heat, then reduce the heat to medium and simmer for 1 minute, stirring occasionally. Add the syrup to the confectioners'/icing sugar bowl. Using a whisk, or with the machine on low speed, blend until the mixture is smooth and all of the sugar has been incorporated, scraping the sides of the bowl with a rubber spatula if necessary.

➡ To glaze, immediately dip one side of each hot doughnut into the warm glaze, and let dry for 10 to 15 minutes before serving.

➡ For glazing tips, see page 29.

CHOCOLATE GLAZE?

There's no such thing as a chocolate glaze. Or is there?

Technically, a glaze is much thinner than an icing and covers a doughnut more thoroughly, dripping down the sides of the doughnut. It's also usually transparent. At Top Pot, we place doughnuts on giant cooling racks as they come out of the hot oil, then transfer them to a glazing apparatus, where we can glaze dozens at a time using a giant handheld glazing trough that allows the glaze to come out in a giant, ribbony sheet.

So no, you don't usually see chocolate glaze—it's usually thicker, and it's called chocolate icing or chocolate frosting. But if you want to make a chocolate glaze, go ahead: add 2 tbsp unsweetened cocoa powder (sifted) to a vanilla glaze with the rest of the ingredients, and go to town.

ICINGS, GLAZES, AND TOPPINGS

SIMPLEST VANILLA GLAZE

SMALL BATCH MAKES ENOUGH FOR ONE DOZEN cake or ring-shaped doughnuts
BIG BATCH MAKES ENOUGH FOR ONE DOZEN large doughnuts (bars, pershings, twists, fritters, or bullseyes)

SMALL BATCH	BIG BATCH	TIME
3½ cups/350 g confectioners'/icing sugar, sifted	4½ cups/1 lb/450 g confectioners'/icing sugar, sifted	5 minutes active time, plus glazing
1½ tsp light corn/golden syrup	2 tsp light corn/golden syrup	
¼ tsp iodized salt	¼ tsp iodized salt	
½ tsp vanilla extract	¾ tsp vanilla extract	
⅓ cup/75 ml plus 1 tbsp hot water, plus more if needed	½ cup/120 ml hot water, plus more if needed	

➡ Place the confectioners'/icing sugar, corn/golden syrup, salt, vanilla, and hot water in a large mixing bowl or in the work bowl of a stand mixer fitted with the paddle attachment. Using a whisk, or with the machine on low speed, blend until the mixture is smooth and all of the sugar has been incorporated, scraping the sides of the bowl with a rubber spatula if necessary. If the glaze seems too thick, add more hot water, a teaspoon at a time.

➡ To glaze, dip one side of each hot doughnut into the warm glaze, and let dry for 10 to 15 minutes before serving.

➡ For glazing tips, see page 29.

MAPLE GLAZE

MAKES ENOUGH FOR ONE DOZEN doughnuts

3½ cups/350 g confectioners'/icing sugar, sifted

1½ tsp light corn/golden syrup

¼ tsp iodized salt

1 tsp vanilla extract

½ tsp maple extract

⅓ cup/75 ml maple syrup

¼ cup/60 ml hot water, plus more if needed

TIME
5 minutes active time, plus glazing

➡ Place the confectioners'/icing sugar, corn/golden syrup, salt, vanilla, maple extract, maple syrup, and hot water in a large mixing bowl or in the work bowl of a stand mixer fitted with the paddle attachment. Using a whisk, or with the machine on low speed, blend until the mixture is smooth and all of the sugar has been incorporated, scraping the sides of the bowl with a rubber spatula if necessary. If the glaze seems too thick, add more hot water, a teaspoon at a time.

➡ To glaze, dip one side of each hot doughnut into the warm glaze, and let dry for 10 to 15 minutes before serving.

➡ For glazing tips, see page 29.

Note: This is a thin glaze, not the thick Maple Icing that is the standard topping for Maple Bars (page 128).

ICINGS, GLAZES, AND TOPPINGS

BERRY GLAZE

SMALL BATCH MAKES ENOUGH FOR ONE DOZEN cake or ring-shaped doughnuts
BIG BATCH MAKES ENOUGH FOR ONE DOZEN large doughnuts (bars, pershings, twists, fritters, or bullseyes)

SMALL BATCH	BIG BATCH	TIME
3½ cups/350 g confectioners'/icing sugar, sifted	4½ cups/1 lb/450 g confectioners'/icing sugar, sifted	5 minutes active time, plus glazing
1½ tsp light corn/golden syrup	2 tsp light corn/golden syrup	
¼ tsp iodized salt	¼ tsp iodized salt	
½ tsp vanilla extract	¾ tsp vanilla extract	
1 tbsp berry jam	1½ tbsp berry jam	
⅓ cup/75 ml plus 1 tbsp hot water, plus more if needed	½ cup/120 ml hot water, plus more if needed	

➡ Place the confectioners'/icing sugar, corn/golden syrup, salt, vanilla, jam, and hot water in a large mixing bowl or in the work bowl of a stand mixer fitted with the paddle attachment. Using a whisk, or with the machine on low speed, blend until the mixture is smooth and all of the sugar has been incorporated, scraping the sides of the bowl with a rubber spatula if necessary. If the glaze seems too thick, add more hot water, a teaspoon at a time.

➡ To glaze, dip one side of each hot doughnut into the warm glaze, and let dry for 10 to 15 minutes before serving.

➡ For glazing tips, see page 29.

Tip: You can use any jam you have on hand—just make sure it's not too chunky, or the color won't spread well, and you'll wind up with goopy spots on top of your doughnuts.

LAVENDER GLAZE

MAKES ENOUGH FOR ONE DOZEN doughnuts

USE CULINARY LAVENDER HERE, WHICH YOU CAN FIND
in the bulk foods section of many large natural grocers.

⅓ cup/75 ml plus 2 tbsp water, plus more if needed

1 tsp dried culinary lavender, finely chopped

3½ cups/350 g confectioners'/icing sugar, sifted

1½ tsp light corn/golden syrup

¼ tsp iodized salt

½ tsp vanilla extract

TIME
5 minutes active time, plus glazing

➥ First, combine the water and the lavender in a small saucepan. Bring to a boil over high heat, and simmer for 1 minute. Remove from the heat, and set aside.

➥ Place the remaining ingredients in a large mixing bowl or in the work bowl of a stand mixer fitted with the paddle attachment. Add the lavender water. Using a whisk, or with the machine on low speed, blend until the mixture is smooth and all of the sugar has been incorporated, scraping the sides of the bowl with a rubber spatula if necessary. If the glaze seems too thick, add more hot water, a teaspoon at a time.

➥ To glaze, dip one side of each hot doughnut into the warm glaze, and let dry for 10 to 15 minutes before serving.

➥ For glazing tips, see page 29.

TOPPINGS

Top each doughnut immediately after it's been dipped into icing. If you wait until all of the doughnuts are dipped, they dry, and the toppings won't stick. The ingredients here top a dozen freshly iced or glazed doughnuts.

SANDY TOPPINGS

With the exception of confectioners'/icing sugar and cocoa toppings, the toppings that follow should be applied to the entire unglazed doughnut, when piping hot. You can place the ingredient(s) in a large bowl and roll each doughnut individually as soon as they're cool enough to handle. In the case of confectioners'/icing sugar or cocoa, place completely cooled doughnuts in a large brown paper bag along with the ingredient(s), fold the top to seal, and shake the bag to coat the doughnuts.

Cardamom sugar
2 cups/400 g sugar mixed with 1 tbsp ground cardamom

Cinnamon sugar
2 cups/400 g sugar mixed with 1 tbsp ground cinnamon

Confectioners'/icing sugar
2 cups/200 g confectioners'/icing sugar, sifted, coat when the doughnuts are completely cool

----

Ginger sugar
2 cups/400 g sugar mixed with 1 tbsp ground ginger

Sugar
2 cups/400 g sugar

Sweet cocoa
2 cups/200 g confectioners'/icing sugar, sifted, mixed with 3 tbsp unsweetened cocoa powder; coat when the doughnuts are completely cool

CHUNKY TOPPINGS

Bacon
8 oz/225 g bacon that's been chopped into tiny pieces and cooked until crisp

----

Chocolate chips or finely chopped chocolate, or candy pieces
2 cups/170 g chocolate chips

Coconut
1½ cups/135 g sweetened shredded/desiccated coconut

Crushed cookies (gingersnaps, Oreos, etc.)
10 cookies

Nuts
1 cup/115 g chopped walnuts, pecans, hazelnuts, or peanuts

Sprinkles/sugar strands, or finely chopped very strong mints
1 cup/240 ml sprinkles/sugar strands, any color

Most ingredients for our doughnuts can be found in large grocery stores. Powdered agar, the stabilizing agent we use for our glazes and icings in Top Pot's bakeries, is available in the bulk foods section of many large natural grocers, as well as at many Asian supermarkets. Look for agar powder (sometimes labeled "agar-agar"), not agar flakes.

Amazon.com

www.amazon.com

Powdered agar, light corn/golden syrup, canned pumpkin, canola oil, confectioners'/icing sugar, gluten-free all-purpose flour, bread/strong flour, chai tea, coconut, caramel bits, sprinkles/sugar strands, cake/soft-wheat flour, all-purpose/plain flour, whole-wheat/wholemeal flour, xanthan gum, all extracts, vanilla, deep fryers, baking sheets/ trays, doughnut cutters, doughnut pans, frying equipment.

Bob's Red Mill

Available at grocery stores throughout the United States. www.bobsredmill.com or 800-349-2173

Gluten-free all-purpose flour, whole-wheat/ wholemeal flour, xanthan gum, baking powder, cornstarch, yeast.

India Tree Gourmet Spices & Specialties

www.indiatree.com or 800-369-4848

Spices, natural food coloring, and fancy sprinkles/ sugar strands.

King Arthur Flour

www.kingarthurflour.com or 800-827-6836 for orders

Cake, bread/strong, all-purpose/plain, and whole-wheat/wholemeal flours, as well as gluten-free all-purpose flour, chocolate, cocoa, extracts (coconut, maple, peppermint), yeast, espresso powder, and vanilla. Limited spice selection.

Mrs. Cook's

www.mrscooks.com or 206-525-5008

Frying equipment, doughnut cutters, doughnut baking pans/trays, rolling pins, candy thermometers, scales, extracts, sprinkles/sugar strands, vanilla, pastry/piping bags, sifters, baking sheets/trays.

Oregon Chai

Available in grocery stores throughout the United States. www.oregonchai.com or 866-972-6879

Liquid and powdered chai tea.

Stone Buhr Flour Company

Available at grocery stores in the Pacific Northwest and California. www.stone-buhr.com

Whole-wheat/wholemeal flour, all-purpose/plain flour, and bread/strong flour.

Sur La Table

Locations throughout the United States. www.surlatable.com or 800-243-0852 for orders

Doughnut sprinkles/sugar strands, doughnut cutters, frying equipment, doughnut baking pans/ trays, lemon and orange extracts, deep fryers, rolling pins, candy thermometers, scales, vanilla, pastry/piping bags, sifters.

Top Pot Doughnuts

www.toppotdoughnuts.com Available at various locations in Seattle, Washington, at Whole Foods Markets in the Pacific Northwest, and at Starbucks worldwide.

Top Pot T-shirts, mugs, dishware, and doughnut information.

INDEX